RED FEVER!

from Rochdale to Rio as 'United' Supporters

Steve Donoghue

Dedicated To
all Stretford Enders
Past and Present
and to the Memory of Sir Matt Busby.
Long Live the Legend
Long Live
M.U.F.C.

SIGMA Leisure

Published by Sigma Leisure - an imprint of
Sigma Press, 1 South Oak Lane, Wilmslow, Cheshire SK9 6AR, England.

Whilst every effort has been made to ensure that the information given in this book is correct, neither the publisher nor the author accept any responsibility for any inaccuracy.

British Library Cataloguing in Publication Data

A CIP record for this book is available from the British Library.

ISBN: 1-85058-415-X

Typesetting and Design by: Sigma Press, Wilmslow, Cheshire.

Cover design: 'The Agency', Wilmslow

Printed by: Manchester Free Press

Not *just* another United Book!

A million football books have been written, thousands of players have published their auto-biographies, hundreds of Managers have their tales to tell and Chairman's memoirs and exploits are ten a penny . . . but what about the people who make the stars, superstars and millionaires worth reading about? Yes – the fans, we know the stars work hard to get that fame, but without someone wanting to watch them perform their art, without the thirst and hunger for information on anything and everything they do, some would still be playing in Salford's back entries or for the local pub team in the shadow of Newcastle's Tyne Bridge – or even kicking the ball between two coats on the playing fields of Glasgow, dreaming of Hampden.

The press wouldn't sell half as many papers, the TV moguls would lose interest if the ratings dropped, and a lot of clubs would go to the wall. No more replica kits, no more executive suites, no more shareholders' dividends, they need us as much as we want them, but no one ever asks us the fans what we think. We helped in many ways to put the clubs where they are today.

This is a book by the fans, about the fans, for the fans, and, I hope will find its way into some players, Managers' and Chairmans' literary collection. It is often said at our club that we must not forget who we are, but the people who run the game are in grave danger of pressing the self-destruct button by becoming too complacent, and may soon damage it beyond repair. We the fans respectfully request they listen to the voice of reason, as it may help rebuild the bond between football and its faithful spectators. These are accounts of what its been like to follow Manchester United as the supporters see it.

Yes, we all now know it took 26 years for our beloved Manchester United to recapture their "Holy Grail" – the First Division (now Premier League) Championship – the precious title all United fans coveted. But how does it feel as a supporter? After waiting all these years, myself and the thirty-odd other reds who have contributed to the book have seen between us hundreds – maybe thousands – of games and we couldn't possibly recollect and report on every one, but we have selected our own favourite moments.

All United fans will have various books and videos on the club's history. The fact that we won The Double in 1994 just had to be included, but this book concentrates on the period from 1967 when the Red Devils last won the Championship at West Ham; when Best, Law, Charlton and the rest of the boys basked in their glorious 6-1 demolition of the Hammers and our fans were in the fountains of Trafalgar Square (not for the first or last time, I may add), up to 1993 when, just like the Kennedy assassination or the moon landing, every United fan on this planet and beyond will remember and tell their grandchildren of the night they were amongst the chosen few who were privileged to be inside the theatre of dreams when all our dreams came true.

Very rarely does it happen when the result is immaterial, but Old Trafford rocked like never before, (except maybe v A.C. Milan and Barcelona in 69 and 84), as we all sang our hearts out for the lads. Our Lancashire neighbours Blackburn Rovers were treated to an exhibition of fine swash-buckling football and a 3-1 defeat, when Giggs, Ince, Pallister and the rest of the team joined in the "mother of all parties" that the fans had started a full 27 hours earlier.

In that time, our club has had its good times and its bad. We may not have always seen eye to eye with the way "our" club has been run, but we've stuck by it through thick and thin and on the whole, yes we do think our Chairman has done a good job. But we pays our money and buy our shares, so we're entitled to our opinions, better the devil you know than the devil you don't, as they say. We just wish the board and Chairman would be a little more open, a bit more approachable and accessible. But we're not here to dig up dirt – just to tell our tale as we see it.

For many of us, we have devoted a lot more than 26 years since 1967, for others, they have not had 'red fever' for very long, but every single one, man, woman and miniature red (child) in this book is a life-long United supporter, no part-timers, no fair weather fans. They are not just punters we've picked on outside Old Trafford, we're all (except for a handful from Crewe) from in and around the Greater Manchester area (just for all you City fans who think we all come from Timbuctoo or the Outer Hebrides) – not that we haven't got a supporters branch there, we probably have!

We are proud of our supporters, whether they travel from Blackpool, Torbay, Norwich or Malta. United have always been around – winning cups, playing in Europe, taking part in the Championship race and most major competitions. They also supply players for International duties at home and beyond our shores, and I'm sure that will continue in the future.

Because of its demise, the Stretford End and the Stretford Enders in particular are mentioned often in this book because most of us who have contributed grew up on that famous terrace. They can tear down the walls and girders but my memories will always remain, and I shall forever be a "Stretford Ender", no matter where I may have to sit in the Stadium in the future.

Joe Jordan, on his move from Leeds to Manchester, was asked on radio to compare Uniteds, to which big Joe replied, "Which United? There's only one United. Manchester United and don't forget it" We won't Joe.

Many thanks go to my wife Elaine for her patience and understanding, my family and many friends who have helped with the research, stories and pictures in the book and have put up with nearly forty years of fanatical dedication to what they call my "one true love" – Manchester United – the club that is not only tattooed on my arm, but engraved on my heart and will be lovingly cherished till the day I die.

Acknowledgements

Thank you so very much for the help and guidance of so many people who helped this project come to fruition, not least: Mike Unger and Kay Sales of the Manchester Evening News; Cliff Butler editor of the United Review; Martin Edwards, Chairman of Manchester United F.C. for allowing us to use photographs in and around Old Trafford; Rev. Jones of St. Francis church in Dudley; Nick Richmond of the Guardian Newspapers London; 'Veg' and 'Zar' and Big John from the fanzine Red Issue; The Department of the Environment and Department of National heritage, Sports and Recreation Divisions; all my fellow supporters who contributed and donated questionnaires, jokes, pictures, various unprintable comments and football songs. And finally, my wife for staying up late into the night with me, re-typing all the re-writes.

Photographic & other acknowledgments:

Manchester Evening News (M. Unger)
The Guardian (N. Richmond)
The United Review (C. Butler)
Scrapbook Album (Steve D.)
Dean Harrison and Steve Ollier
Prime Minister's Office, Downing Street
Department of Environment
Department of Health

The use of all photographs, trademarks and suchlike items are my complete responsibility. Efforts have been made to trace copyright holders of all material used in this book and I apologise for any omissions which are sincerely unintentional.

Cartoons and Jokes

Veg and *Zar* of Red Issue, plus fans' own contributions.

Fans' own contributions in alphabetical order:

Andy 10 foot	Little Hulton Reds
Angela	Salford Reds
Andrew	Stockport Reds
Big Andy	Swinton Reds
Bed the Red	Farnworth Reds
Bill	Eccles Reds
Boothy	Clayton Reds
Captain Chaos	Wigan Reds
Chris	Roe Green Reds
Crazy Horse	Salford Reds
David	Bolton Reds
Deano	Ramsbottom Reds
Denise Red Bird	Westhoughton Reds
P. Moores	Heywood Reds
Graham	Little Hulton Reds
Griff	Prestwich Reds
Herbie	Sale Reds
Ian	Blackley Reds
Ivan	Crewe Reds
Jardine	Tyldesley Reds
John	Wythenshawe Reds
John Snr.	Bolton Reds
Jud & Jean	Little Hulton Reds
Kev Red Eye	Westhaughton Reds
Marion	Salford Reds
Olly	Crewe Reds
Paul	Manchester 9 Reds
Peter	Moston Reds
Popeye	Walkden Reds
Red Shark	Salford Reds
Saul	Salford Reds
Steve	Clayton Reds
Tasmanian Devil	Salford Reds
Wado	Crewe Reds
Win	Ardwick Reds

Bibliography

Six Years at United, Alex Ferguson (pub: Mainstream)

The Quest for Glory, Tommy Docherty (pub: Sidgwick & Jackson)

Steve Donoghue

Contents

1

WHO'S THAT TEAM THEY CALL UNITED?

How does the song go? *Walking down the Warwick Road to see Matt Busby's Aces.* But in the early '60s I had to walk the mile or so from the club's traditional heartland of Salford, down Cross Lane, past the docks and over the Trafford Road swing bridge before I could sing it. I've lost count of the number of times I've trodden that path, the times I'd skipped and jumped as a youngster, laughed and cried as a teenager, staggered (after a few shandies) in joyful bliss or utter disbelief at what I had seen as a married family man – although now I usually drive down the lane, trying to keep off the path.

We all have to start somewhere and, with most fans, it's usually by supporting the team their father, grandfather or uncle would like them to follow. But some of you with split allegiances in your family will know that isn't always the case – you know, where mum's a Red devil fan but you are a sky Blue; dad likes Spurs, but you like Arsenal (unlikely, but possible); or heaven forbid – calm down, calm down – Aunty Mary is a Liverpool fan but you have a fondness for the toffee men in blue. With hindsight, I think all young fans should *play the field* when it comes to watching football, because to love the beautiful game as a fan, you have to appreciate its various aspects. Too many young fans are so blinkered that it can be harmful.

There's nothing wrong with a bit of rivalry and

Welcome to The Pleasure Dome! Old Trafford.

pride in your team, as long as you know where to draw the line. Throughout this book, what I have written about our Blue neighbours across the city is just friendly banter and all in the *best possible taste*. Every club has its own individual style, tactics and flair, or lack of it, and the more you see, the more you appreciate the game. The individualism of teams, fans and grounds make football the beautiful game it undoubtedly is.

How many times have you been at a match and thought: "He's having a good game" and then the bloke a few yards down shouts: "He's as much use as a chocolate fire guard"? It's all about individualism. Obviously, I try to influence my children in their choice of team, but for one reason or another it doesn't always work out. You see a great goal, have a great day out at a match, enjoy a little bit of magic by one player in particular. When you were a kid, it could be something as simple as the kit your team wore, or seeing fans celebrating on TV and imagining yourself in the crowd. But although any fan loves his or her team, I don't know one real football fan who doesn't have a soft spot for another team.

The whole point to this is to answer the question: Why United? Well, for me it started with walks through Weaste Cemetery. My gran would say: "See on that stone there? He was one of the *Babes* who played for United", and I would wonder: "Who's that team United". Every time we took flowers down to my great-grandma's grave, I would see this stone with the name of one of the *Babes* – Eddie Colman, a local lad who made well.

On with the Red and White

I may have seen the Busby Babes as a toddler but I honestly can't remember. I do know that I was taken by my proud parents along to OT (Old Trafford) before I was five or six years old. You only have to look in the United Review programme to see that babies as young as four weeks were being brought to the stadium. In Salford it was tradition: as soon as baby was home and settled, it was on with the red and white and off to the game. As I grew up, I went with my grandad and dad. One week we would go to see United at home, and when they were away we would go to White City dog track or Belle Vue Zoo, or the Cliff to see the youth team. That was it – I was hooked.

But my earliest memory of a game was the first of the 1963-64 season, versus Ipswich. I've

kept the programme – with Noel Cantwell on the front holding that famous FA Cup trophy – to remind me of the day. What great timing, because I can say to my grand-children: "I saw him" – the boy genius who became, for me anyway, the most talented footballer ever to grace Old Trafford's hallowed turf. Yes, on the 14th September 1963, along came *El Beatle* himself – George Best.

Surprisingly, my first encounter with a footballing superstar up close – close enough to talk to and not just shout for on the field – was not a United player, but Sir Stanley Matthews. This was at his home near the Squires Gate area of Blackpool in the mid '60s. Two or three of us went there while on holiday – it was a big corner house with a tennis court and, I think, a practice putting green at the side with steps leading up to the back door.

His wife or housekeeper – as a young boy I didn't know who she was – let us wait knowing he wouldn't be long. When he came home, he invited us in to see his trophies and have a quick chat, being very modest about his own career. I told him I was a United supporter and he agreed that Matt had some good boys in his teams. He spoke generously of Edwards and Colman, Charlton and more, just as my grandad had done, and told us a few things about the trophies in his cabinet. I kept his autograph on a scrap of paper for years until, like most small boys, I lost it.

But now, 30-odd years later, it all comes flooding back. I hadn't given it a thought until now but, as a young impressionable lad, Sir Stanley's words reinforced dad and grandad's stories about United. Although my dad was actually a Glasgow Celtic supporter, he did go and see United now and again. I was lucky as I got the best of both worlds growing up, seeing two of the best teams around in that era – Best, Law and Charlton every other week and Tommy Gemmell, Jimmy Johnstone and Bobby Lennox two or three times a season when my dad took me along on a special occasion.

As I said earlier, nearly every football fan has a soft spot for one team or another. I always enjoyed games against Forest, West Ham and Sunderland, because of the style of football they played. Burnley always had to sell their best players, but they still played attractive football in the '60s, and I still look for the results of Wolves, Wigan and Torquay for reasons long forgotten, and Celtic's for obvious reasons.

But by the time I was big enough to join the *Miniature Reds Mafia* down at the dockside, with the age-old question: "Mind your car mister?", I was well and truly a Manchester United nut. All kids around most major grounds did that, to help pay their admission and for the bus fare home. I did it to get in the Stretford End and to buy tyres for my bike, but these days car parking is big money – walkie talkies and security guards.

Great Victories

Over the years since 1967, I've seen some great victories that bond a supporter to his team: the 6-1 win over West Ham was marvellous. I remember staying in a hotel near Euston Station with my dad, and how we celebrated with the hordes of United fans passing our hotel. We ended up dancing in Trafalgar Square, before I retired to bed again dreaming of the goals from Law, Herd and Best.

The 1967-68 season was party time in our household. It was another trip down to London, and this time my dad bought a van for £1. He took me, my uncle and some other pals and we had a great time. I can't remember much about the game, but I do remember Georgie Best's goal and the band playing *Congratulations*. It was just one of those nights when everything was so exciting – it flies by in a blur.

In 1970, United played Northampton in the FA cup. The genius George Best got six goals in the 8-2 victory and Brian Kidd also got two. I remember United fans up trees and on the roofs overlooking the small and muddy ground. I've never seen so many goals scored by one player, and the papers were reporting "Six of the Best" the next morning. I know it was only little Northampton, but to score eight goals against any club in any competition is a great achievement and for one player to get six of them in a cup tie was something very special. That's why the match-winning ball can be seen in United's museum.

The last match of the season in 1971 was away at Maine Road, versus City. We had an awful season, but we did get to the semi-finals of the League Cup against Aston Villa. Though the Derby was one to forget, I remember the goals from Best (2), Law and Charlton in a 4-3 win: sweet revenge for the 4-1 defeat at home earlier in the season.

In 1975, United won the 2nd division in style. But the season started for me by working in London during the '74 World Cup. I had arranged to meet my friends at Euston Station for United's

first game at Orient, which was why a load of Arsenal fans thought I was travelling in the wrong direction for the game! I wore a plain red and white scarf – the black band still wasn't in every scarf at that time.

When I got to Euston, I heard "United, United" and I ran up the escalators with excitement to see my friends, only to see a crowd of chanting West Ham fans. I ran down the up escalator like Linford Christie, I can tell you, then an almighty roar went up as the United special train arrived. The police sorted out the trouble makers and me and my mates went to a bar near the Post Office Tower before making our way to the Leyton Orient ground and saw United win 2-0.

On to 1976. One of the best atmospheres I've experienced was in the semi-final of the FA Cup against Derby County at Hillsborough. I don't know if it's the shape of the ground, but United always create such a noise when playing there, it's electric. As the game continued, the Derby fans were leaving and the United Red Army's colours of red and white were spreading right across the terraces. By the end of the game, we had virtually taken over the whole ground.

Gordon Hill's second goal was greeted with "We shall not be moved" and, on TV later, I remember Brian Moore saying he had never heard a noise like it. We saw him outside the ground before the game in a lime-green jacket – it blinded you, and that was some 15 years before raves and fluorescent colours were invented. United won 2-0 but for once it was the crowd I'll remember, not the game. I even saw fans wading and swimming across the river that runs parallel to the ground – they were so determined to get in.

Also that year we played Wolves in the 6th round. We drew the first game 1-1 at OT and set off for Molineux three days later, for the replay. The train broke down just a few miles from the station and with only 20 minutes to kick off someone said: "I know the way to the ground" and about 490 of the 500 on the special jumped down on to the tracks while the guards were shouting for us to stay on the train.

I'll never forget a woman's face as we all climbed the embankment into her back garden. She was ironing and nearly dropped the iron in fright. Within minutes, police cars and vans were escorting us to the ground and we managed to get in about 15 minutes after kick-off. It was a hard game with goals from Greenhoff, McIlroy and Pearson, and United won 3-2 and 4-3 on aggregate.

1977 was a brilliant season with some great games and top scores of 5-0, 5-4 and 7-2. There were cup ties against Tranmere, Sunderland and Newcastle, and European soccer trips to Holland and Italy. It was rounded off with a trip to Wembley in the FA Cup against Liverpool, having beaten Leeds in the semis again at Hillsborough, and gaining revenge against Southampton for their cheeky win in the cup the previous year – I still say it was off-side! The first game at the Dell ended 2-2 and the Saints fans invaded the pitch, but turned back at their penalty area when they realised the United end was open for business, so to speak. United won the replay 2-1 to go through to the next round.

That's the Ticket

The final came, and many thousands made the journey down the M6 without tickets – even with tokens, the tickets were swept up and were like gold dust. An average £3 ticket was going for £30 or more. We hired a mini bus and set off after last orders at the pub on the Friday night. Of 16 of us, four – including myself – were ticketless. After sleeping in the minibus on Wembley's car park all night, a quick bacon buttie and a game of footy at breakfast, the hunt was on for spare tickets.

After a few hours, the fans were arriving – singing and smiling, tickets held close to their chest in fear of being mugged. Then, we saw a Wembley official coming in and out of the main box office and into a small wooden shed, selling tickets to fans from both Manchester and Merseyside. We thought this was terrible – ripping off fans for £20 a throw, but even this was cheaper than the touts.

I went up to two police officers and told them what was going on and asked what would happen if we went in there and took the tickets from him, and just gave him face value. They said that as long as we didn't use unreasonable force they would turn a blind eye, so my mate and I waited for the official to come out again. Two Glasgow Reds who were waiting before us got their tickets and we were next, but the official in the peaked cap never came back out again. I wonder why?

After that, we walked around asking anyone and everyone for spares, but in vain. Then, outside the Wembley Esso Hotel, we saw City's Tony Book and Dennis Tueart. Things were getting desperate and we asked Dennis if he could

get us in the hotel to watch the game on TV. He said: "I think all you lads should get into the final, it's a shame" and disappeared inside. To his credit he came back out 10 minutes later and said that if it was up to him he'd let us in but the boss had said no. He tried to track down a couple of spare tickets, but no joy.

By this time the four of us had split up and it was 2.20pm. I could hear all the Reds inside singing and I saw some lads getting in through a window on a rope, but then I saw this old boy with a peaked cap standing alone looking lost. I asked him twice if he had any spares and he said: "No, son". I kept an eye on him and he never moved, so I went up and asked him again. "Third time lucky", he said, "I'm waiting for my nephew and he's not turned up. If I give you his ticket, you won't re-sell it will you?" I told him that at 25 minutes before kick-off, he must be joking. I rummaged in my pockets, scraped together £30 and held it out to him. But all he wanted was the £3.50 face value. I gave him a fiver and all my copper and told him to get himself a pint at half-time, then flew off not believing my luck.

We all know the result, 2-1, and it stopped Liverpool and their expected treble, but on the Queen's Jubilee special occasion, who else would you expect to win? – of course, the Red Devils. Afterwards, I found out the other three lads had seen the game on TV – one saw it in the car park on a portable plugged into a car battery. The other two knocked on the vicar's door near the Greyhound pub entrance. He gave them tea, and those "little devils" acted like angels going without beer and swearing and bought the vicar's wife a box of chocolates for letting them in.

Game, what game?

In 1978 we had a great day out at Carlisle. Joe Jordan had just joined United and was behind us in the stand, but it wasn't Jimmy Greenhoff being sent off or the result that stayed in my memory. Just before Carlisle, we came off the motorway, drove along the A6 and stopped at a pub called the Three Crowns. We were greeted by a wonderful landlady who welcomed United fans in her establishment – at the time, most were turning football fans away.

A few pints went down, a few games of arrows by an open fire and the landlady's home-made hamburgers. We nearly didn't leave for the game – "Game, what game? – let's have another pint". Yet we had to go and a few miles up the road a Luton van passed us making an awful racket. No wonder, as there were about a dozen Reds in the back with the roller door up and a blow-up sex doll flying about, tied to the padlock latch, with a United scarf around its neck. It was hilarious – the Reds were singing their heads off and banging on the sides of the van, what a sight!

Also that year, we played F.C. Porto in Europe. I remember sitting up in bed in the early hours listening to the match report – it was terrible. We went down 4-0, and from that day to this I can't bear to listen to a United game on the radio if I'm not actually there. On the night of the return leg, the atmosphere in the Stretford End was awesome. United fought like the devils they are named after – they scored five goals, and we all thought they were going to do it. Porto got another late goal to go through 5-6 on aggregate, but what a night!

Just before half-time, it was my turn to go for the beer. On my return, with three full pints, I carefully negotiated a packed Stretford End, got back to our group and, just on the stroke of half-time, Jimmy Nicholl scored a screamer. All three pints went up in the air, right over the head of one of the ladies in our group. Picture, if you will, somebody wearing a face pack – that's how this lady looked, except it was beer-based! She forgave me and, if she's reading this all these years later, she'll remember it I'm sure.

On to 1983. United have played some great Cup Finals, but the one against Brighton was a cracker, and on Sir Matt's birthday as well. My mate and I went down on the train and, as most fans who have been to Wembley will know, there is a great big Courage pub just before the ground. So we hopped back there on the tube, had a few beers and raised a glass or 10 to all the Reds arriving on the other specials that pulled up at the pub, queuing up to disembark at Wembley.

We decided to get a taxi back to the stadium and we were stood outside hailing black cabs when along came a Rolls Royce with a seagull on the roof where the aerial should have been. Two suited gentlemen said they were lost and offered us a lift – sack the chauffeur! We chuckled, because as United fans we knew our way blindfold and, for the price of a glass of champagne, we duly directed them – arriving at a Wembley Cup Final in a limo fit for royalty was great. You should have seen the people's faces as Brighton and United fans got out of the same car.

Happy Birthday, Matt Busby

"Glory, Glory Man United" was ringing through the rafters that night as we won 4-0, the biggest winning margin in over 80 years and to cap it all, Sir Matt Busby was on our train on the way home. What a reception he got from the fans when they realised the great man was in the station – "Happy Birthday, Matt Busby" echoed across Piccadilly station. We visited Wembley four times that season.

In 1985 the film *Ghostbusters* was in the cinemas and United fans adopted its signature tune as *Scousebusters* as we beat Liverpool in the semi-final at Maine Road. We went on to beat Everton with 10 men at Wembley and won the FA Cup yet again. But the semi-final goals by Bryan Robson and Mark Hughes sent the Blues' ground into raptures, and the volume of noise that night hadn't been heard since we used to play there in the war years. One of my mates from Chadderton lifted Robbo shoulder-high, and he needed a police escort to leave the pitch.

Just before the Cup Final, I was painting a new date on my flag for the final in the garden, when I heard of the Bradford fire and ran in to switch on the TV. I watched the horrors of that fateful day but I add with pride that Manchester United were the first to offer support to the Yorkshire club with a charity match. Our fans raised a tremendous amount of money at the Cup Final for the victims fund. 1985 was infamous for another football disaster but for very different reasons, and that's why the terrace wars must stop.

Merseysiders

In 1988, United were getting a mauling from our arch-rivals Liverpool at Anfield. This is never an easy fixture, but one I enjoy attending. As I went to sit down, I bumped into Paddy Crerand who obliged with a photograph. During the game, the fans never gave up: we were behind our team all the way, putting paid to the claims from the kop: "You only sing when you're winning". That was all we heard from them after they scored because, until then, we were making all the noise. But then, up popped Captain Marvell, Robbo again, and he got a goal with not a single defender within yards. Grobbelar didn't even smell it and I've got a picture of it from the stand to prove it.

We went wild as McClair and Whiteside got two more to make it 3-3 and the chant went up:

"You'll never beat United". The fans and the players knew we had a brilliant psychological edge and, at the end of the game, we stood on our seats and gave the whole team a rapturous standing ovation. What we hadn't reckoned on was Fergie sending the players out to lap the pitch. We were pleased with the fight back, especially as it was away from home, but I've always wanted to ask Fergie why he did it, because the players must have been exhausted.

The 1990s are well documented elsewhere in the book – there were trips into Europe and beyond. And there are hundreds of stories from the mid-60s to tell – of games against City, Spurs, and Chelsea and with players that included Bell, Doyle, Greaves, Gillsine, Harris, Cooke and Osgood. But the real story in this book is from 1967 onwards.

So there we have it, just some of a lifetime's memories and the reasons why I picked United as my team. These days we fans walk down the Sir Matt Busby Way and, much as I think the name is well-deserved, we will always be "Walking down the Warwick Road" and my team will always be Manchester United.

250,000 welcome United

T HE GODS came back to earth last night untouched by human hands but bruised by an estimated quarter of a million throats.

Matt Busby and Manchester United were protected back into Manchester in a cellophane wrapping of security arranged by British Rail, several hundred police, and an open-topped double-deck bus. The welcome home for the European Cup winners was a well ordered affair based on the old principle of "look-but-don't-touch."

The journey from London was archly traced by British Rail announcers at Manchester's Piccadilly station. "The special train from Euston"—could there be any other?"—was on time at Rugby, Stoke . . . " and so on up the line. The special bus was waiting for the special train. The approach road to the station had been closed 1½ hours earlier. Only bona fide travellers were allowed on the precincts.

A bona-fide traveller, a BR policeman explained, was someone not wearing a red-and-white scarf or rosette. When the train pulled in, the team

By our own Reporters

were transferred, unhampered by supporters, to the bus waiting on the platform. Two security guards heaved what looked like a hat box on board. Out came the European Cup.

The bus moved out into the city. It seemed a thin crowd, 'no more than four deep on the approach to Piccadilly. But the war chants rumbled incessantly : " Yew-night-ted." " We are the champ-yuns."

In Piccadilly the statue of Queen Victoria—not as well protected as that of her consort

further down the road—featured a banner announcing her a Stretford-ender. As the 3 mph Triumph moved down Market Street, Albert Square in front of the Town Hall was swollen with the " Wilson out. Busby in " Stretford-enders.

The bus arrived at the town hall in a whirling kaleidoscope of scarves, faintings, police horses and a climactic moan, half exultant, half adoring. " We shall overcome—Georgie —Matt—United—We shall not be moved."

May 31, 1968: Reproduced by kind permission of *The Guardian*

2

I'M THE MANAGER NOW

It's a doddle!

Is it difficult being the boss of a club like Manchester United? "Narrr, it's a doddle," I hear a lot of fans saying. "They should be on our wages, stuck behind a welding mask building train carriages all day, or standing in footings (building foundations) up to their ankles in clay and rushing to get the brickwork finished before frost and snow set in".

We just have to look at poor Wilf McGuinness and his shiny dome, or the way that the England manager's hair and features change totally in front of our very eyes – no turnip jokes please – to realise it's difficult. The pressure is enormous, but I bet there's not one of us who hasn't picked the team for the manager, signed or substituted "that useless twonk" a thousand times over, on the terraces or down the pub with our mates. And there's not one of us wouldn't leap at the chance to be the manager or chairman and think ourselves privileged to have had the opportunity – just for one single day.

In the time I've been following the club we've had seven managers. In my opinion, there were three great ones who, for different reasons, the fans took to their hearts. Sir Matt, the Doc, and now Fergie have steered the club through some of its most historic moments. Fans have their own favourite for particular reasons – maybe the younger or more recent supporters weren't around in the '60s, '70s or '80s. I wish I was old enough to have seen Delainey, Carey and Edwards at their peak in the '40s and '50s, but that's life. We hear stories, read books and – fortunately – have them on film to admire at our leisure.

Three Great Managers

Sir Matt Busby

Where do you start to say anything about this phenomenal gentleman? I wouldn't dare to presume I was eloquent or worthy enough to tell you or anyone else about his football and managerial record – that speaks for itself. I can only relate the encounters that will stay with me for the rest of my days.

In the '60s, as a young lad like thousands of other Reds, I had seen Sir Matt at the ground many times. We swarmed around him in the hope that the great man would give us an autograph or a glancing smile. I was able to pat him on the shoulder as he aimed for the players and staff door near what was the family stand – previously the Scoreboard Paddock – yet others would go through the commissionaires' double doors under the main stand.

Like some star struck groupie who had just touched her favourite pop singer, I'd say: "I'll never wash this hand again. Did you see, did you see? I touched Matt Busby's arm". Then, we would all go to his Jensen Intercepter – looking through its windows, polishing its paintwork with our scarfs, because anything the great man touched was sacrosanct, cherished and coveted by the fans.

In 1968 I was in Blackpool to see Sir Matt turn on the famous illuminations. I had a great spot, right at the front of the scaffold stand where the lights were switched on, waiting since about 5.30pm. By the time Sir Matt and Lady Busby came out, Talbot Square was a mass of singing, swaying fans, and smiling faces. Sir Matt went through the usual formalities and then said: "I've brought something for you all to see tonight", and as he pulled the lever to turn on the extravaganza, a spot light shone on the European Cup and the crowd went berserk.

Fireworks and rockets flew up into the sky. I had to stand on the scaffolding and crane my neck to see the festivities behind me, not realising I was then just two or three feet away from the Cup and the man they had all come to see. I couldn't resist it. I just reached out my hand and caressed it and Sir Matt saw me. Just for a split second, like a kid caught with his hand in the cookie jar, I expected to be reprimanded by him. But he just smiled as if to say: "Go on son – it's as much your cup as it is mine, I won it for Manchester United and the people". It was either that or: '' Yes son, one more step and I'll box your ears". I prefer to think the former – the memory I shall keep forever.

One other occasion that comes to mind was just after United won the FA Cup in '83. I went down to the ground mid-week for no reason in particular. I nearly always have my camera in the glove compartment in case I see any players or something unusual at the ground. This was just as well because, as I was browsing in the souvenir shop, Sir Matt came in. I stood there gobsmacked when he came up to me and said: "Are you alright son?" in that deep Scottish brogue. I asked for a photograph of the two of us together, and he kindly obliged.

I felt immediately at east in his presence – a warm friendly man. I chatted to him but mostly I listened, as many a player and manager has done over the years. I could see how he commanded such respect from his old players, who say they would run through brick walls for him. Just a few minutes in his company was one of the biggest thrills in my life. He must have met countless numbers of fans and probably this meeting meant nothing to him, but to an ordinary fan it was a magical moment.

We were inside Old Trafford in the players' lounge and there it was, the FA Cup, gleaming silver. It's funny, but it looks a lot smaller than it does in pictures or on TV. It has a kind of blue glint in the silver when the light shines on it, but don't you City fans go getting any ideas, the only blue you'll see on that cup is if we have to play in a changed strip. I looked at the cup and thought of all the great captains who had hoisted that trophy aloft in the club's name: Carey, Cantwell, Buchan and Robson.

I asked if I could do the same and I was told to get on with it, but not to drop it. I got about four or five shots, one with my scarf wrapped around it, which I also keep in the car – talk about flying the flag! It doesn't take much for me to whip it out and wave it around, I can tell you (my scarf! my scarf!). That's just what I did to Ian Rush, waiting at the traffic lights in Liverpool. We looked at each other, and I just picked up my scarf, kissed it and showed him the club crest's Red Devil. His smile turned to a blank expression – no rude gestures from either side, we just drove off our separate ways.

One more brief tale. The word on the plane on the way home from Rotterdam was that, before the kick-off, it was getting a wee bit hectic outside the main stand in the pouring rain. The queues had merged and security was non-existent but, when Sir Matt arrived, the scuffles and abuse receded and the previously uncontrollable crush parted for the great man to enter the stadium. United, Barcelona and Dutch fans alike spontaneously applauded his entrance – that was the measure of the respect in which the fans held him. I can't imagine anyone else who could have achieved that feat at a Cup Final.

I said earlier that whatever I could say about Sir Matt would be all too inadequate, but these are just some of the comments from others:

"Matt Busby's without doubt the greatest manager whoever lived. I'm not saying I think he's the greatest manager, I'm saying he is the

Sir Matt Busby. In addition to a knighthood, his honours included CBE, Hon. Freedom of the City of Manchester, Knight Commander of St Gregory

greatest manager. I think many men have gone to Matt for advice and he's an inspiration to everyone". – Bill Shankly

"Given the chance, I'd rather manage Manchester United than the England team". – Brian Clough

"The biggest disappointment I had in football terms was I regretted that I didn't take the job at Manchester United when offered, after Sir Matt retired". – Jock Stein

"He will be remembered forever as the father of modern day football. Thanks to him, Manchester United have become more than a football club, they are now an institution. In '56 he paved the way in Europe for others to follow and created some of the greatest teams ever to grace the world of football". – Tommy Docherty

As the saying goes: "How do you follow that?". After writing about the great man, everyone else pales into insignificance, well almost.

The following poem was a late addition to this chapter and I hope you will share in a tribute to the great man Sir Matt Busby – born 26th May 1909, passed away 20th January 1994.

Stars Shine in Your Eyes

From the Lanarkshire mining village you came
To bless this our beautiful game
Known to one and all as Matt, no airs and graces
From the lowest to the high.
To do what you have done
To see what you have seen
The rest of us can only but dream.
You have made us what we are today
For what you gave, we can never repay
Decades of joy and heartfelt pleasure
Sacrificed, blood, sweat and tears
Which can never be bettered.
We saw you dance on that balmy May night
So many players have shone in your eyes
Delainey, Carey, Edwards, Pegg and more
Charlton, Best and the king Denis Law.
From player to president, loyal and true
Humble, gallant, strong and fair
There are no fairer words your people can give
Similar great men will welcome you there
And when you look down upon your
Theatre of Dreams you will know
From here to eternity
Manchester United will be our team
In all our eyes you will always be seen,
And the legend you built will never die.

Tommy Docherty

My memories of the Doc are in a totally different vein. He was never a man to mince words or be short of a rhetorical quip. I've only spoken with him on Piccadilly Radio's phone-in and in '77 outside the Royal Exchange in Manchester. I asked him to stop the Scousers' treble and he replied: "We'll do our best son, we'll do our best" – which they did.

When we were relegated in 1974 after the Derby game, he said: "It won't be easy getting back here. They'll want to keep us in the 2nd division for the revenue. When you leave Manchester United there's only one way you go – down – as a manager or as a player. Now it's time to make a prediction. I've never been as certain of anything in my life: this club will return next year to where it should never have left – the First Division".

And that's exactly what they did. United bulldozed their way through the 2nd division. They were top of the table virtually from beginning to end, and only lost seven games all season out of the 42. Doc's Red Army broke attendance records the length and breadth of the UK. Crowds of up to 62,000 at OT were back in vogue and were remarkable. He brought back swashbuckling football with two wingers, Hill and Coppell, even though it was with Gillette twin-blade razor adverts.

United bounced back first time – more like rocketed back. We didn't languish there for eight years, or yoyo up and down like some do. And that's why the Doc won our hearts. His team played the United way – open, fast, attacking, exciting, classy, cool, calm and collected at the back (except for Paddy Roache) and devastatingly effective up front. Many a time the chant went up: "What's it like to be outclassed" and "We shall overcome some day".

The Doc came close a couple of times to fulfilling the fans' dream. The *Holy Grail* was in sight, but just out of reach. We got to the FA Cup Finals in '76 and '77, and I swear to this day – the more times I freeze-frame on the video – that the Southampton goal was offside. Although we stopped Liverpool and their dream of a treble, they didn't reckon on Stuart 'Pancho' Pearson, Macari, Greenhoff and others – the Doc just ran out of time.

The summer of '77 was a wonderful one for most Reds. The major news stories were about a dictator in Uganda called Idi Amin, the Queen's

Tommy Docherty, the Manchester United manager, consoles the Liverpool players as they flop down in the middle of pitch waiting to receive losers' medals.

Docherty's day but a time to shed tears for Liverpool

Cartwheels at dawn without an audience

Frank Keating

Though he could have fooled me, Tommy Docherty said he had been soberly restrained during the runaround at Wembley with the Cup. This was his fourth final at the place and he had yet to leave it as a winner. Let alone his defeated visits with Scotland. So he reckoned that when he finally made it he would "dash about like a grinning mad thing turning cartwheels all over the place". But in the event he said he had felt a deep sense of anti-climax and just wanted to "go sit in a corner and think 'Have I really done it?'"

He could have fooled us, for after a touching handshake for each of the slumped, sad Liverpudlians he turned into a cavorting near-dervish round the pitch. Even watching again on the television one saw he could not keep his hands off the Cup — and if one of his players borrowed it for just one tiny feel he gabbed the lid or the base for another rub. And, unlike ex-President Ford, he managed to do six things at the same time — rub, pose, grin, chatter, give eight-page interviews about it being the

players' day, and still chew that gigantic wedge of gum

And though the party went on into the small hours the amazing fellow was, by all accounts, up in his tracksuit not long after dawn for a morning jog in Hyde Park. And there, appropriately near Speakers' Corner, it apparently started to sink in and there did the Doc do his cartwheels. It was all the more real and relevant too, because the wee nutter usually likes to do this sort of thing in front of an audience.

It was the end of a lovely day. There were, of course, a few arrests before and after but nothing like the number that had been feared. Obviously the Cup final is considered a sacrosanct day out to even the most harebrained Red Army supporter. Like, apparently, the Kray brothers who would always kneel in the right pious places when they attended a family wedding. Hymns by the crowd and tackles by the players were never as dirty either as most Saturdays in the year. Indeed, some of the banners were most original (GREENHOFFS GO IN RUSHES, HO!) though for my

money the best remained the classic—JESUS SAVES AND PEARSON NETS THE REBOUND.

The turning point for many in the Pressbox was Stepney's first-half wrong-way save from Kennedy's marvellous header (from a distance on high it had even the flickering feeling of Banks v Pele in Leon) but on Saturday night Stepney said he had never smelt it, not a touch, it had nicked the post even though a corner was given. The nice old goalkeeper admitted he had lain down and cried at the final whistle — just as he had done, for different reasons, at the very same time last year. He played jolly well, more for his wise owl, totem-pole effect on the youngsters, though once or twice with a couple of butterfingers and a rash back pass or three he might have thought he was dreaming back at Millwall all those dozen years ago and swearing at the like of Harry Cripps.

FA CUP FINAL: David Lacey-

—Manchester United 2, Liverpool 1

Silver Jubilee and Elvis's death. None was particularly eventful in football terms, until Monday 4th July 1977, when I was holidaying in Torquay. I left the girlfriend in the guest house to go and get a paper. I couldn't believe my eyes! I stood in the newsagents reading every single headline, totally out of my head with the shock of it: The Doc was gone. No matter what you may think (as a Red or a Blue) of the Doc these days, don't be too hard on the old boy. Deep down, he's still a die-hard Red and many of us remember those swashbuckling teams he produced.

Just a footnote to the story: While we were in Torquay, a nun used to sit opposite to us at breakfast. I found out she'd been in Africa for 40 years, had returned to the UK and was having a wee break before returning to her convent. We chatted each morning and, at the end of the week, she told me that one of the sisters in her convent was from Manchester and that they prayed for Manchester United every morning. She didn't explain why and she didn't know I was a Red. Surprising isn't it? Reds are here, Reds are there, as they say.

Alex Ferguson

Fergie, as we all like to call him, is a different kind of animal. The media give us the impression he's a cross between Taggart and Rab C. Nesbitt: a tea-cup-throwing temper, a sharp tongue and steely stare. Obviously, the fans at first weren't close enough to the man to understand his character. I have met him a few times and he does resemble the Glasgow cop somewhat. I once asked him to sign *Taggart* underneath his autograph, but he graciously declined saying: "Och away, I get enough of that from the wife. She thinks I'm like him as well".

On a more serious note, we all know Fergie had a hard time when he first arrived. The fans were anxious and amazed at some of his team selections and substitutions, and I must admit I was one of them. But I felt that we couldn't keep changing managers every time things didn't run to plan – give this bloke a chance to settle in. When someone near me started shouting the customary abuse, I would start up a song or a chant that would catch on and drown him out. It

"My job is to turn the dreams into reality" — Alex Ferguson's first words in the club's 1986 membership annual.

European Cup Winners 1968.
Semi-finalists 1956/1957/1958 and
1969. Competed 1994.

ECWC winners 1991.
Competed 1963/64, 1977/78,
1983/84, 1991/92.

Premier League Champions,
1993 and 1994. First Division
Champions 1908, 1911, 1952,
1956, 1957. Second Division
Champions 1936, 1975.

**Some of the trophies
on view in the
club museum**

GLORY
MAN

Pride of Manchester cup. Since
1985, United won this trophy so
many times that the cup was
presented to the club to keep.

Five Manager of the Month, 1992/1993/1994 and
two Manager of the Year, 1993/1994, awards

FA Cup Winners 1909, 1948,
1963, 1977, 1983, 1985, 1990,
1994. Finalists 1957, 1958, 1976,
1979.

League Cup Winners 1992.
Finalists 1983, 1991, 1994.

European Super Cup Winners
1991. European Fairs Cup
competed 1964/65. UEFA Cup
competed 1976/77, 1980/81,
1982/83, 1984/85.

GLORY UTD!

Lancashire Football League
Winners, 1993. FA Youth Cup
winners 1953, 1954, 1955, 1956,
1957, 1964, 1992. Finalists 1982,
1986, 1993. Lancashire FA Cup
Winners 1994.

Charity Shield Winners 1908, 1911, 1952, 1956, 1957,
1983, 1993. Joint holders 1965, 1967, 1977, 1990

didn't work all the time, but I timed it right more often than not. Football crowd humour was along the lines of: "Did you know Fergie's token sheet goes 1, 2, 9, 16, 4", but we could see things changing for the better when we got to the semis versus Oldham. Alex Ferguson would be the first to admit he nearly got the sack in his first three years.

I phoned my uncle in Paisley to see if he knew anything of our new boss's character. He said he'd spoken to Fergie a few times up at St Mirren and he always had time for the fans. He'd stop and chat, even to Celtic fans, when he was a Rangers player. If he could do it for Aberdeen, he could do it for United.

Okay – that's only the opinion of a supporter, just as mine is. "Who does he think he is, to characterise a football manager?" I hear you say, but we all stereotype people we don't really know. After that call I was more open minded. The fans could see changes, the players were training harder down at the Cliff, the youngsters were budding Maiorana, Beardsmore, Robins, etc., new haircuts were in all round, club blazers and so on. Let's give credit where it's due, Fergie turned this club upside down and gave it a damn good shake-up from top to bottom.

He transformed it, signed up new coaches, had scouts running around up and down the UK, involved more local schools and got the club back into the community. But I would like to see the club do a bit more for the Greater Manchester Supporters members – more player appearances, dinner dances and better away ticket allocations. And how about more closed circuit TV matches if we are only to get a small allocation of away tickets?

Fergie has brought back that *never say die* attitude to the club, like the great United teams of old, with old boys like Kiddo, Nobby, Jimmy Ryan, Pop Robson and others – people with a good reputation. With some of them being ex-Reds you know they'll give their all, as we the fans do. There's one thing you can depend on: if the supporters like a player or a manager, they're treated like gods. But if we don't like what we're served up, we'll soon let them know in no uncertain terms.

Since our boss has put his own stamp on the club, we've won every major honour possible in English football and more: the FA Cup '90 and '94, Charity Shield '90, E.C.W. Cup '91, European Super Cup '91, League Cup '92, FA Youth Cup '92 and the Premier League Trophy in '93 and '94. Plus, of course, winning The Double in 1993-94! In

the Charity Shield 1993-94, we came close twice, and were League Cup Finalists in '91, and the players have won player and young player of the year awards on a few occasions – not a bad catch after an initial spluttery start.

I have a couple of memories of Fergie that I will cherish for ever. In Rotterdam, when everybody was going ape – leaping around, screaming and singing their heads off after the presentation – I saw Fergie give Sir Matt a peck on the cheek. I'd love to know what they said to each other. Then he came on to the pitch and with a smile as broad as a Cheshire cat, started orchestrating the fans with an invisible baton – it was like the last night of the proms, only better. Something like 30,000 to 35,000 Reds, much more than our official allocation, and every single one of us sang to the timing of Fergie's finger tips – absolutely marvellous.

The other time was when Stevie Bruce scored his two late, late goals against Sheffield Wednesday in April. He and Kiddo flew out of the dugout on to the pitch, Kiddo on his knees, praying – well he was at the Mecca of football – and Fergie punching the air, yet not knowing whether to invade the pitch or not. The whole stadium was going absolutely crazy with delight. Later that evening the boss was on *Match of the Day* saying: "There's only one point in it, there's no way we're going to get carried away about it" and immediately after, the credits ran with Kiddo and Fergie doing it all over again – an absolute gem for Dennis Norden's *It'll be All Right on the Night*.

There's a lot been said about Eric Cantona's signing making all the difference this season. But, as we all know, one man doesn't make a team, as we found with Robbo – the team adapted and learned to do without him for long periods. In my opinion, Lee Sharpe was the lad who did it for me: he came back at the right time and got stronger and fitter as the season went on, along with Giggsy and Ince, who have improved and matured so much it's unreal. I'm forever arguing that Paul has lost his *Whingeing Ince* tag, since he's got his head down and shut his trap. It's paid off by getting the captaincy of the National team, so all you Blues and lads down the pub, get the salt 'n' pepper out and eat your words.

I think Fergie's finally getting the appreciation he deserves, and I'm not just saying that because he's finally brought back home the Holy Grail to where it belongs. I've not always agreed with all his or the club's decisions, but as he said in his book about Archie Knox and Brian Kidd: "We have arguments, of course, but that's one reason you have an assistant, to assess the pros and cons of problems".

I started off not knowing much about Fergie. Now, having read his book and learned to appreciate his style of management – if not his sense of choice and timing of substitutions – over the years, I'd like to wish him all the best with his own personal goal of: "Finding the perfect team, a side capable of going through a whole season undefeated". And hopefully in Europe, too, but that's another story yet to come, isn't it?

At the end of Fergie's book he says: "I am manager now, in the true sense of the word. I accept I have been on a learning curve, an apprenticeship if you like. I wish I could go back five years, knowing what I know now, and when I hear the supporters chant *Ferguson's Red and White Army*, it gives me a feeling of immense pride and inspires me to achieve the vision Sir Matt Busby always had for Manchester United".

A ticket tout's dream! Left to right, top to bottom: World Cup Final, Spain 1982; European Cup Semi-Final, O.T., 1968; European Championships, Italy, 1980; World Cup, 8th round tie at O.T., 1966; European Cup Final, Wembley, 1968; ECWC Final, Rotterdam, 1991; League Cup Final, Wembley, 1992; European Super Cup, O.T., 1992; FA Cup Final, Wembley, 1983; UEFA Cup 1st round tie, Amsterdam, 1976; Charity Shield, Wembley, 1977; New Year's Day Derby, Glasgow, 1984; Premier League Championship v. Blackburn, O.T., 1993; Bobby Charlton Testimonial, O.T.1972; Closed Circuit TV, live from Plymouth, 1977

3

A PART-TIME SUPPORTER? NEVER!

Those were the days my friend we thought they'd never
*   end*
We'd sing and dance forever and a day
We'd live the life we choose and fight and never lose
Cos we're the Stret, we are the Stretford End.

I still can't believe it is no more, but like the phoenix it has risen again from the ashes, and I hope to God as many of the old guard as possible have managed to get back in the new *Stret* and the newcomers will try to make it as gloriously colourful and noisy as it ever was.

When I was younger, any time I had a day off work or during the summer, I'd get withdrawal symptoms and just had to go down to OT and stand on the Stretford End, all alone, and take a panoramic view of the place. I'd re-live games and see the legends of the club ghost past the halfway line, pass superbly to the central area of the box, for numerous goals to fly in from all angles. And then I'd just stand there and do a muffled roar as the phantom ball strained against the netting after it had flown in at an unstoppable angle, day dreaming of a packed swaying mass – the Stretford End at its best.

Over the years some Stretford Enders have got to know each other's faces, standing in the same part of the ground for years – some making it their second home. We've queued out there for hours in all weathers, waiting for the gates to open – a time when queues became non-existent because so many were trying to get in. It was just a tide of red and white people, all pushing and shoving but in a friendly way.

Many's the time I've made it to the front without my feet touching the floor, face upwards, gasping for air in the crush and excitement to get in. We'd pass young kiddies over our heads to the front, be chivalrous to young women shouting: "Move back, push back", to stop them being

crushed and be shameless to the pretty ones that caught our eye, doing what Roma fans have been doing to female tourists for hundreds of years.

I've even gone to the game on crutches with a broken leg while fans parted like the Red Sea, for me to gain entry. Twenty-odd years later something similar happened that you will have read earlier with a sense of *déjà vu*. We've queued for Cup Final tickets under it, around it, in our thousands, reading every bit of graffiti dating back to the '40s: Fred the Red on the ledge, Law is King under the girders of the staircases. There was Six foot two, eyes of blue engraved on a turnstile exit door and even my own Dono from Salford scratched deep into the concrete crash barrier on the left side.

To the uninitiated, the Stretford End was divided up by the fans long before the fences and barriers went up. Originally most of the left side of the crowd came from the Salford area because of its proximity to Warwick Road and the United Road entrances, and the right side and the paddock came over the bridges from the Stretford areas. The front was generally for the lads, juniors and young girls wanting a better look at their heroes and the central area above the tunnel was for all the young guns, the hard core rebels – call them what you will.

The Heart of the Stret

Most of us started at the heart of the Stret and as you got older you worked your way gradually to the sides or into the stands and seating areas. In our time Manchester United supporters and the Stretford Enders in particular, as well as the fans in the Scoreboard Paddock, United Road and the now infamous K Stand, have been worth a goal start. We've scared rookie players out of their wits, sucked in goals, been praised to high heaven and disowned to damnation. We've roared till we were hoarse and laughed and cried, felt ecstasy and despair, but whether you love us or loathe us we are undoubtedly some of the most loyal and devoted fans you'll find anywhere.

United fans now come from all over the world, but even back in the mid '60s, they were known to come from South America, Russia, Poland, Italy and Malta. I remember this foreign looking guy standing next to me when one of Bobby Charlton's rockets just missed the goal by a whisker and it hit this poor fella smack bang on the nose and knocked him senseless. Sheffield Wednesday game mid '60s, I think it was. This poor chap's nose resembled Henry Cooper's after the Clay fight, and people helped pass him down to the first aiders at the front. I wonder what story he took back home to his foreign land.

A lot of grapevine gossip has passed football fans' ears over the years, about fans taking this or that end, kop or terrace. We all remember the bad old days – pubs and shops with boarded windows, waiting in anticipation for what may and,

unfortunately, sometimes did happen when rival sets of fans clashed.

Stretford Enders earned a reputation that preceded them. It grew and grew, until at one point at least one national newspaper wanted us banned from not only the Cup Final but every ground in the country. But the true fact is, that the majority just wanted to see United play anywhere, any time, and some of the smaller clubs and towns had never seen the Red Army on manoeuvres and just couldn't handle it. Many's the time we've walked down High Streets and seen kids and old ladies waving from doorsteps and upstairs windows. We've ended up giving our scarfs and hats to them in the pubs and cafes. The minority who caused the bovver got all the media attention

Up until the mid '60s fans could stand side by side. At the game, of course, the odd scuffle would break out, but it was usually sorted among the fans before it got out of hand. But as time went on it became more and more unacceptable for away fans to come and stand on home turf. Between the 30 or so of us in this book, those who have been standing on the Stretford End all these

The old Stretford End, filling up nicely some two hours before kick-off

years can only remember two occasions where trouble had flared on home turf.

The first and only major disturbance of its kind at Old Trafford was in 1966 versus Everton, where hundreds of Scousers packed into the front corner of the terrace. The first aiders and police earned their pennies that evening – the hordes were repelled and restrained, but it was very hairy indeed. From that day to this, no supporters have ever been allowed to share the Stretford End in any large numbers.

The second incident was minor compared to the one of '66. It was the Derby versus City in '74 when United were relegated and was one of the most emotional and highly charged games ever played at Old Trafford. Denis Law The King, who scored the goal for City to win 0-1, has since said he is glad he didn't score the goal that relegated us to the 2nd division, but no matter the score at Old Trafford, Birmingham's results would have done the same anyway.

As we all know, that was the only goal The King ever scored after which he didn't make his famous one armed salute. It was his very last kick of the ball in league football, because he left the field immediately, and even then United fans ran on and consoled him and hung red scarfs around his neck. After all, to us he was our king and always will be. I dread to think what would have happened if one of the others had scored.

Anyway, it sparked off an invasion of the pitch from the Blue corner of the main stand due to the fans in the Scoreboard Paddock surging forward. It was like holding up a red rag to a bull – I wonder if that's where the nickname comes from? The fans in the Stretford End erupted like a champagne cork – there was no going back. Like a tidal wave breaching the sea walls, all hell broke loose and it was all over.

Clubs and Football, Hand in Hand

In the late '60s early '70s, I used to attend all nighters in the Northern Soul scene: American soul music venues like the Twisted Wheel in Manchester; The Torch, Stoke; Blackpool Mecca and Wigan Casino – they and football went hand in hand. You may think they had nothing to do with football but you are wrong.

People, mostly from the mods and skinhead eras, attended these events and their favourite football clubs over the weekend. But even though United and City, Stoke and Port Vale, Blackpool and Preston, and fans from all over Lancashire and Yorkshire used to attend the all nighters, we would all mix happily enjoying the music and live artists from America. In the 15 years or so I was around the scene, I never saw one fight or any major trouble. People tell me the raves of today are the same.

The Stretford Enders were a great crowd – the terrace humour at times crude but no worse than at rugby or boxing. Often the noise and atmosphere created by United's Red Army bordered upon mass hysteria and hopefully the stories in this book will help you bring those memories flooding back. Like the beautiful blonde streaker we had under the stand at half time in the '70s who made at least three flying visits past us before the police even cottoned on to her whereabouts.

And the two old grannies in E Stand (Stretford End seats) who hit the sergeant with their walking sticks when he tried to make them sit down and stop shouting abuse at a Leeds player who was giving Georgie Best a bit of close man-to-man marking. And the cheers that erupted as the sergeant made a discrete exit. I bet that wouldn't happen these days.

A little more up to date, who remembers the day when a young girl popped out of the crowd and sang karaoke in the Stretford End? She sounded more like Madonna than the original and we all craned our necks trying to see who this voice belonged to. One thing led to another and she was helped by Stock, Aitken and Waterman and actually released the Pointer Sisters number called: "I'm so excited . . . it's Man United". Yet another first for the Stretford Enders.

With 26 years' worth of memories in the theatre of dreams, there are a million and one stories to tell and we could fill a book on its tales alone. I'd like you to read a small piece from the United Review for the last game of the '92 season, about the King himself, Denis Law.

The King

There may have been several pretenders to the throne, but there was only ever one king. Denis Law arrived here from Italian club Torino, in the summer of 1962, and he immediately became a firm favourite with the Old Trafford crowd, and in particular the Stretford Enders, so much so that in no time at all he was crowned King.

Undoubtedly one of the all time great players, Denis recently took time out to have a last look at the famous terrace. "Running out to play in front of these fans was terrific. They really are the best in the business. It was like a shot of adrenalin when you heard the Stretford End roar. I was honoured and flattered when they adopted me as their king and I shall never forget them".

United fans have been in some of the biggest and most famous football stadiums in the world, but none of them had the intimacy or feel of the Stret. They were either so big they lost the sense of belonging or too sunny or too wet in the open air. Some terraces were so steep it was too dangerous to sway around or we were so high up the teams looked like Subuteo players or ... well, a hundred different reasons spring to mind – it just wasn't home.

The Red Army's regulars on manoeuvres get to know one another. Impossible you may think, but over the years you get to see the faces – there's a sense of camaraderie. In every day life you could be a top lawyer or a bin man – it doesn't matter, away from home we are all Reds on tour, and a Red is a Red, and that's all that counts.

To be in the Stret on a warm summer's evening at a big European game with a packed house, hearing the roar, singing till it felt like your lungs were fit to burst was an awesome experience. To be part of a cult following as a Stretford Ender with a worldwide reputation was and still is a great buzz.

Among my Souvenirs

At the end of the '92 season they demolished the Stret and I went down for a few souvenirs. I was after the turnstile plate from gate 52 which I had been going through religiously all these years. Football fans are superstitious just like players and managers. We are all creatures of habit – many fans liked to stand in the same spot every week and get to know everyone around them. Some wore their favourite scarf, hat, badge, tie, jumper – anything they thought would give Lady Luck a hand in many games.

Anyway, I got my solid brass plate, a gate number 68 with May 29th scratched into it and the Stretford End sign above gate 52, some bricks and squares of turf. I would have hired a van if the wife would have let me, but she threatened a divorce if I came home with a complete turnstile. You don't know how close a decision it was petal – just kidding.

19

But I wasn't the only one down there. One of the demolition men told me: "Blokes have been coming down all week. One chap took enough bricks to build a wishing well to wish United good luck". (It worked in '93). And, as we chiselled off the brass plates, a Japanese Red emerged smiling from ear to ear holding up his spoils – a toilet sign. He was chuffed as mint balls

My pride and joy – my scarf is older than most present-day players:

but we didn't have the heart to tell him what it said.

The club did tear down the walls, but every little piece is scattered about in homes and gardens all over the world, and will be a cherished prize for countless fans. It has gone, but my heart will remain there forever and there will never be another like it. A part timer? I think not.

These are just some of the metal badges fans can collect home and away

4

REDS ARE HERE, REDS ARE THERE

Manchester United fans will go to amazing lengths to see their team. I have hitch-hiked to games on the back of coal wagons, builders' vans, a Harley Davidson, in the back of a bread van and once even in an ambulance. I've cadged my way on to all-nighter fruit and veg and mail trains, arrived in style in a limo and even traded things to get transport to see my team all over the country.

When United went to Rotterdam I heard stories down at the pub that a couple of Reds held a car boot sale to raise money, selling such things as exercise bikes, stereos, sofa beds and a washing machine. You'd need a damn big car boot to get that lot in, and I wondered whether they had any furniture left at home and whether their wives knew they were selling them. Now there's a thought: you could imagine the blokes coming home to the old rolling pin reception, saying: "Oh luv, it was magic, the goals, the fans, the trophy, brilliant". Smack! Oh yes, worth a night in hospital don't you think?

"Reds are here, Reds are there" is often chanted at the games up and down the country and abroad. We never cease to be amazed at the distances United fans will go to see their team. If Manchester United were to play on the moon we could probably boast we'd have fans there also.

I heard Tommy Docherty once took the team to Africa in the mid '70s and they were asked to play a friendly way up in the mountains. After a few hours on a dusty track with cliff hanger drops they arrived in this village and the first people Tommy and Gordon Hill saw as they got off the coach were three young black kids totally naked except for their United scarfs singing: Oh Tommy, Tommy, Tommy, Tommy, Tommy, Tommy Docherty and Gordon Hill's King of all Cockneys.

How the hell did they know who they were? Incredible!

More was to come. When they got to the ground a crowd of more than 25,000 was there waiting to see the Reds, having come from all the surrounding villages in the mountains and in the middle of the African jungle. Reds are here, Reds are there or what? I've seen Brazilians, Dutch and Cypriots by the dozen; Scots, Welsh, Germans, Italians and French Reds down at OT by the coachload; Irish, Scandinavians and Maltese by the ferry and plane full. I've seen the Americans, Aussies, Japanese and Russians yeah, the real Red

Army, arrive at Old Trafford, all proudly sporting the colours of Manchester United Football Club.

The first tour I wanted to go on was the European away semi final tie versus Real Madrid back in '68. After seeing the first leg at OT, very few people gave us a chance with only a 1-0 lead. I really wanted to go to the famous Bernabeu Stadium but as I was only a school kid with a paper round, there was no way I could afford the 25 guineas = (£26.77) and even if I could, my dad wouldn't have let me go alone. And my grandad didn't fancy going to Madrid because he didn't like the . . . how can I put it? . . . the spicy food Europeans ate, and the wine. Not exactly the same as a good pint is it?

The Come-back of All Time

So I had to make do with the radio reports from the BBC and Radio Luxemburg. It was great to hear that the few thousand Reds who made it to the 120,000 crowded stadium were not going to be stopped from congratulating Bobby and the boys for what was claimed at the time to be the come-back of all time in the European competition. A 3-3 draw thanks to Big Bill Foulkes, of all people, made it a marvellous 4-3 aggregate win and we all know what happened just 13 days later in the final against Benfica.

Over the years I've travelled thousands of miles watching the Reds, sometimes with only a few bob to spare in my pockets. I've gone without food and a decent bed for the night to see my team, bunked down in railway stations, camp sites, slept on beaches in Italy, just as long as I got a ticket for the game and the fare to cover my return journey. I've been to Holland, France, Italy, Spain, Denmark, Greece and the other Reds in the book have seen the Red Devils in Hungary, Poland, Russia and Portugal as well, so between us we've been all over Europe in the 'crusades'.

United had a barren spell in Europe from '70 to '75 while they got their act together. I mean, how do you go about replacing a legend as manager? It's not an easy task. Anyhow, the board went for another Scot, Tommy Docherty, and he got us back on the rails and set Doc's Red Army loose again on the worldwide crusade in search of the Holy Grail.

This time it led to Amsterdam home of Ajax. It was 1976 and my first chance to see United abroad. On the ferry all the lads were looking forward to a good game with the Dutch. Card

schools were out, the beer was flowing, the steak and chips on the boat were selling like it was out of fashion because we reckoned we wouldn't get a chance for a good meal for the next 12 hours. We'd be too busy drinking and having a good time around the red light district we'd all heard about. Not that I would partake of the Ladies of the Night – we just wanted to see what all the fuss was about.

By the time we arrived on the outskirts of Amsterdam we'd made up a song called Last bus from Amsterdam (see 'songs' chapter). Stopping at some traffic lights I spotted a beautiful blonde on the central reservation wearing a dark fur coat. She opened it to flash us nothing more than black lace undies and suspenders. When I pointed this out to my mates who were pre-occupied with looking for the stadium's floodlights they nearly trampled me to death, tongues tripping them up against the steamed up windows of the coach. "Hello Eeenglish, pretty Eeenglish boys". The cry went up: "Stop, stop the bus!" but this time for a very different reason. Let's just say some of the guys never got to see the game.

United played in all blue with a white stripe on their shorts. They played well enough, though not brilliantly and we thought Stuart Houston scored just a minute into the second half. We were all leaping up and down on the so-called seats, which were actually benches with numbers painted on them. But as it had been raining during the day and we were in an open end and nobody sat down anyway. The ref disallowed the goal. Krol scored for Ajax and a 1-0 deficit was not too bad to take back to OT.

Doc's Red Army was again on the move. We'd made a few pals on foreign soil, swapped scarves and hero stories, and on the way home, upon sighting the White Cliffs of Dover, it seemed every fan on the ferry was up on deck singing the Rod Stewart song Sailing – a floating Stretford End. They were all over the lower and upper decks, in the life boats and in front of the bridge. What a sight! Even the captain came on the tannoy and said: "I've heard a lot about Manchester United supporters but I'm glad to say you've been great ambassadors for your club and country. We haven't had a single complaint from any of my staff except that the duty free has run out of beer". By the way United won the second leg 2-0 and went through to the next round.

In 1980 my mates and I went to the European Championships in Italy, travelling the whole length of the west coast from Turin, Pisa, Rome,

Naples and back up to Pisa. Despite all the trouble, we had a great time because we were based near Pisa and travelled up and down the coast by train. We went to a few games and watched others in the hotel bar on TV.

United fans seem to be well represented in all the countries of the British Isles whenever I've seen them, though I can't speak for the Welsh. I should imagine with Ryan Giggs, Mark Hughes and Clayton Blackmore in their squad they must have some United followers among the ranks. Italy '80 was not all tear gas and batons, the staff at our hotel were very friendly and we made friends with all the locals in the bar we frequented the most in our resort.

Knock, Knock, Who's There?

On our way to Naples we stopped off in Rome to visit the Colosseum and the Vatican. A friend of our hotel manager was at Pisa station and was on his way to Rome on weekend leave. Being in the airport police he carried a gun which he showed us more than once on the train. He told us how Naples was like John Wayne City with shootings between police and Mafia. When we got to Rome he kindly offered to show us around.

As it was very early in the morning, about 5 o'clock, the sun was just up and the streets fairly quiet. He flashed his ID and we all got on the metro free, and again in the Vatican, where we went down into the cata-combs and corridors underneath St Peters. The priests were all singing morning prayers – it was a marvellous place with all the paintings, marble and gold leaf.

On the outside one of the other lads knocked on a massive door, obviously not realising the Swiss guard were on the other side. They opened the doors to reveal a huge staircase with all the dif-ferent corridors cutting across from both sides. As the police officer was

explaining our ignorance to their customs, his Holiness Pope John Paul II and all his entourage passed the staircase on about the fifth level. It was only a fleeting glimpse but you can imagine this guy going home to Stretford and telling his mates down the boozer: "Knock, knock, who's there? The Pope" honest.

Once in Naples, we saw an incident that led to over 200 fans on our train being so disgruntled that I wrote to Mrs Thatcher in protest when we got home. As we know, English fans are blamed for most of the trouble caused at international games – sometimes justified. But the majority don't go for the trouble and this incident in the Napoli stadium was a case where they got the blame though it was others who caused it.

England were playing Spain and the fans were mixing with the Italians at the other end of the ground. Down in the corner at our end along the touch-line was a small number of Belgians – about 100 or so. The game passed off peacefully until about 15 minutes from the end, when a large number of Spaniards started walking round to our end but the Belgians were between us and them. A few scuffles started, and the Belgians were being pushed into our end, very dangerously being squashed against fences and gates. The England fans could see what was going on and started helping the Belgians stuck in the corner over the fence and gates.

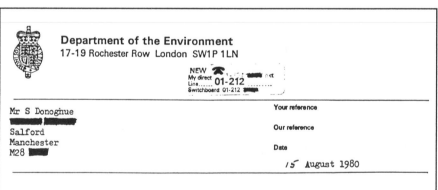

Department of the Environment
17-19 Rochester Row London SW1P 1LN

NEW
My direct 01-212
Line
Switchboard 01-212

Mr S Donoghue

Salford
Manchester
M28

Your reference

Our reference

Date

15 August 1980

Dear Mr Donoghue

Your letter to the Prime Minister of June 23rd concerning the recent crowd troubles at the European Championships in Italy, and the many problems facing the English supporters, has been sent to this Department for reply.

Unfortunately, it is always the case when these incidents occur that the actions of a few will tarnish the image of the majority of supporters. Letters such as yours and independent reports do indicate that much provocation was suffered, but we understand that there was a small element who used this to excuse their subsequent behaviour thereby letting all of you down badly.

Mr Monro, the Minister for Sport, is having talks with the FA about the special problems of matches abroad, as it is clear that the UEFA seeks regarding the control of rival supporters, ticket sales etc. need to be closely adhered to, especially at games that give rise to such high Nationalistic feelings.

I thank you for having taken the trouble to write explaining the problems which I appreciate were great.

At this point the Italian police waded in. Instead of asserting their muscle at the Spanish fans' area, they over-reacted with the England section and, though I personally saw Belgians thanking England fans for their assistance, all we saw on TV later was an England player and other officials disowning the fans for their actions. I was so annoyed I wrote to Mrs T and my MP saying it isn't our Prime Minster who should be apologising to the Italian parliament, it should have been them apologising for the way we were treated. Okay, some hot heads went to town but most of us were there to have a good time and enjoy the footy.

United are a World Club

When it comes to Internationals, I like to keep an open mind. Although I'm a Lancashire lad and have stood on foreign soil singing Land of Hope and Glory for the lions of England, I've also sung Flower of Scotland with the Scots, Danny Boy with the Irish and even Italia Amore with the Romans in Spain when they played the Germans in the World Cup Final '82.

I go to the football for the football, and to have a good time, win, lose or draw, no matter who's playing. It's old fashioned I know, but if one country is knocked out of a competition, I will support any of the five nations from the British Isles who are left in it, especially if there are any United players in the squad. I have the greatest regard for the Scots, Irish and Welsh – after all, their players and managers in particular, have served Manchester United well over the years

Think about it before you shout abuse at certain players when they're having a stinker of a game at OT. Meredith, Davies, Hughes, Giggs (Wales), Law, Crerand, Holton, Buchan, Morgan, Macari, Albiston, Jordan, McClair (Scotland), Carey, Delainey, Whelan, Gregg, Cantwell, Dunne, Best, Daly, McIlroy, Moran, Stapleton, McGrath, Keane, Whiteside, Irwin (Ireland, North and South) and not forgetting Jimmy Murphy (Wales), Sir Matt Busby, Tommy Docherty, Alex Ferguson (Scotland), Frank O'Farrell and Tommy Cavanagh (Ireland). Put them along with all the other brilliantly talented Internationals we've had and still have, and you'll see it's ridiculous to be biased at the game.

United are a world club and it would be unfair to shout only for Manchester or English born players, like our neighbours do – those days are long gone.

Thinking of brilliant players from Manchester and England. How about trying to pick your all-time favourite Manchester United team from all the players listed on these two pages, along with all these English players. Woods, Stepney, Bailey, Rowley, Mitten, Roberts, all the babes, Viollet, Berry, Taylor, Edwards, Colman, Byrne, Johns, Pegg, Foulkes, and Charlton. Stiles, Herd, Sadler, Kidd, John Aston Snr and Jnr. Stan and Stuart Pearson, Brian and Jimmy Greenhoff, Coppell, Hill, Wilkins, Robson, Bruce, Pallister, Parker, Ince, Robins and Sharpe. Any club in the country would be glad to have any one of the 70 in their team, and there are many many more players from overseas you could choose from.

In 1982 me and the guys went to Spain for the World Cup Finals and saw Manchester United players make the headlines yet again. The fastest ever goal in the history of the World Cup – Bryan Robson's goal versus France came in only 27 seconds. And Norman Whiteside became the youngest ever player to play in the finals at the age of 17 years and 1 month, beating Pele's record.

We saw England, Scotland, France, Brazil, Italy and West Germany games in the tournament and stayed on to see the final in Madrid. It was like the United Nations on our coach. We had a Man United white ensign on one side window of the bus, another Scottish rampant lion, a MUFC flag on the back and the Northern Irish lads had their flag up. Three Dutch blokes were up near the front while a dozen Spaniards and three or four Italians filled the coach.

All the British lads on the bus, who were well used to away matches, got on kitted out with carry outs – beer, pop, butties, fruit, toffees, papers, cards and the obligatory girlie mag to pass around – while most of the others sat there parched and quiet. The back half of the chara was rocking and one little Italian fella told me that it would be: "The besta daya ofa mya life" if Italy were to beat the Germans later on that evening, and if they won he would buy us champagne.

A Dream Came True

We arrived in Madrid and it was like a mass carnival especially when a group of Brazilians came dancing down the main avenue. It seemed all the representative countries' fans were there whether their teams were knocked out or not. Finally a dream came true, for me anyway.

Fourteen years earlier I'd desperately wanted to see United play Real Madrid in the second leg of the European Cup semi final. Never back then in '68 did I ever imagine I'd get any further than Blackpool to see a United game, yet here I was in the magnificent Bernabeu stadium. I decided I was going to follow Italy in the final after England, Scotland and Brazil were knocked out of the cup.

From Russia with love: wet and cold with warm vodka, before the game with Torpedo Moscow

Italy won the World Cup thanks to a chappie called Paulo Rossi, later to put a stick in the spokes of United's European ambitions, but for now, he was the talk of the town. Back in the coach, the little Italian fella danced up the isle in the car park and on the way back to our hotel we stopped at a restaurant in the middle of the Spanish desert and, true to his word, he bought a whole crate of champagne for all the lads on the bus. And because I'd given him a Vienna roll earlier in the day he insisted on paying for my T-bone steak.

Being a United fan as we all know gives us the chance to see some of the greatest players around, too numerous to mention. But the theatre of dreams has been the stage for all our boyhood heroes. It gives you the taste for more, and that's why we love to go on manoeuvres into Europe and beyond to see United pit their wits and skills against the rest of the best in the world.

We are simply the best – it says so on all the souvenir shop carrier bags, badges, stickers and so on. Having seen the best Europe could offer in the way of football there was only one continent left for a couple of foot soldiers of the Red Army to explore and seek clues to what makes a team

good enough to capture the Holy Grail – South America.

A couple of Reds I know went off to the Mexico World Cup in '86 to see Robbo, Wilkins, Strachan and Co. But they came back with stories of street riots, shootings, beggars and overwhelming heat and exhaustion. They did tell us one amusing tale where a pair of beach buggies were seen heading for Mexico City with a couple of flags flapping around on the back with Rochdale Reds and Ashton-under-Lyne Reds M.U.F.C. on them. Trouble was they were hired on Acapulco beach for the day – over 300 miles away in the other direction.

In 1988 a couple of us had sacrificed the Mexico tour to save up for the trip of a lifetime to Rio de Janiero to see the real thing in the Maracana stadium. Most people's idea of the most naturally gifted players on earth are the Brazilians and to see the home of Flamengo and Flumanasie was too good a chance to miss.

Don't go getting the wrong impression: we were just a few ordinary working class blokes who had saved up, taking on extra part time jobs to raise the money. It took two years in the planning. Like most things in life, you have to sacrifice other things to get what you want, and we did. Manchester United fans could teach Thomas Cook and The Holiday Programme a thing or two about budget holidays. But no amount of glossy brochures or street-wise common sense can prepare you for the third-world experience that places like South America, Asia and Africa can bring.

Rio is, without doubt, the most beautifully natural geographical place I have ever seen, but its neglect and downfall since the European influence left is incredible. You can see the Portuguese and American style hotels and architecture all round you – massive pink buildings, swimming pools with statues and cherub fountains. The only trouble is it's falling to bits. I don't think a single building in Rio isn't corroded or has had any maintenance carried out for 30 or 40 years since its heyday in the '50s.

On our first visit to the world's biggest football stadium, we thought we'd go on the terraces like at home. Oh tish, a bad move! We headed for behind the goals of the home team Flumanasie, but as we got close up to the front half a dozen seats, we heard a lot of whistling behind attract-

The Maracana stadium, Rio — biggest but not necessarily the best.

ing our attention. Some guy came down and told us to move back quite a few rows so we did. Just then I spotted a vendor selling soft drinks and hot dogs, so I got the order in for all the lads and noticed he was wearing a builder's hard hat – like the Stretford Enders used to wear, painted up, in the late '60s and early '70s.

As I got back, the teams and officials were coming out on to the field of play and at that point the vendor went scuttling off up the stairs el-rapido, as the biggest, loudest firework bombs went off. It shook the terraces – all four of us wondered what the heck was going on when beer cans, fruit and plastic cups came raining down

from the tier above, right on top of the first five or six rows where we were originally sitting.

It was 0-0 at half time and we decided to take a look around at the stadium. Our 90p light blue seats close up were very rusty and the terraces hadn't been swept in years, all in all a bit of a disappointment. The crowd too was only a measly 25,000 plus – this is a ground that only two weeks before we arrived had held over 210,000 for the Tina Turner pop concert. It didn't show the place off to its full extent. Your Real Madrids, Barcelonas and so on don't always get 100,000 plus gates every week and over a whole season Manchester United's overall attendances are very favourable compared to all the other big clubs around the world. For constant loyal support we're a hard act to follow, and if United had a larger capacity stadium I'd wager we'd fill it more often than not.

One thing happened in Rio that, believe it nor not, has stuck as tradition and used to happen in English football in the old days: when the team changed ends at half time so did the fans. Yeah, I know it's incredible but they go round clockwise down two subways so they don't clash with each other and up they pop on the other side with flags and samba bands ablazing all over again. We stayed put but it was an amazing sight. Could you imagine United and City changing ends at Old Trafford or Maine Road?

With all our excitement none of us can remember the opposing team but apart from a few individual touches the game was pretty average, a 1-1 draw. But in Brazil you always see a winner because they have penalties at the end so one or the other team goes home happy with a win.

The next game we chose was the big boys of Flamengo and the best supported team in Rio, we were told. Outside the stadium we were looked upon like aliens from another planet. We unfurled the Manchester United flag and wrapped it around the statue of the Brazilian player holding up the Jules Remet World Cup they got to keep back in 1970.

We went in the best seats, at £3, an enclosure of clean cream coloured seats with cushions on them, with 10-foot high fences on either side and armed guards every 20 feet down to the pitch. It was really strange – this was obviously the rich, mainly white's paddock. As 90% of the fans on the other side of the fences were coffee coloured, poor people from the *fervellas* (ghettos) this was a culture shock to our system.

The Maracana stadium is so huge that they had VW police vans driving around the roof keeping an eye on the crowd. Right next to our enclosure was one of the many 25-piece samba/ salsa bands famous at the World Cup matches wherever Brazil play. This game, too, seemed pretty average stuff ending in 2-2 draw and it went to penalties. This was when the fun started – arguing with ref's decisions, play acting goalkeepers trying to put players off their shots and so on. Well the home team lost on penalties and their fans with their huge flags on poles started to move round to where the referee's tunnel was.

Two armed guards with rifles guarded the tunnel and both linesmen covered and shielded the referee as he left the field while a mob threw old fruit and coke bottles at him as he waved goodbye.

One more tour was in 1991 – United's European Cup Winners Cup Final in Rotterdam. Manchester United's official ticket allocation was 17,000. Barcelona, believe it or not couldn't accommodate all their allocation of 17,000 we were told, and the rest of the stadium was a neutral zone given over to the Dutch supporters. But when we arrived at the Feyenoord Stadium, thousands upon thousands of Reds had made their own way there having obtained tickets from other agencies and sources. All in all we reckoned there must have been between 25 to 30,000 plus Reds in that ground on that horrible wet and blustery night of May 15th.

Nothing and nobody was going to stop us winning this trophy if the fans had anything to do with it. Eleven official chartered plane loads took off from Manchester, another six from Birmingham and nine more from London, and every scheduled flight into Amsterdam from Ringway had queues a mile long. Over 100 coaches left Old Trafford and the City centre for the ferry crossings and at least that number again set off from supporters' club branches all over the UK and Ireland.

Ooh er missus, that's a big 'un: Reds on the plane

When on away matches, it's good to see where all the coaches come from, with their United supporters' branches painted on placards and flags, hanging in the back windows. Our coach driver at Amsterdam airport told me nearly every single coach firm in the North West was hired to bring fans from Manchester, Salford, Wigan, Stockport, Rochdale, even Liverpool and Chester.

The Red Army on manoeuvres in Rotterdam

The car park, or should I say closed off duel carriageway alongside the sea port, they had set aside for us had hundreds of coaches parked up – it seemed never ending. We'd all had a drink and decided to write our coach name and number on our arms so we could find it after the game. It was well organised. By about 6.30 the ground was filling up nicely and we were bumping into well known travelling United fans who we'd come to recognise over the years. The Blackpool Reds are well known to travel everywhere watching our boys – and the Torquay crew and the Barnsley branch.

The game kicked off and for the next two hours it was pure bedlam. The wind blew hard, so the Red Army just pumped up the volume. The rain came down so we just did a rain dance and the conga up and down the seats. Stop, here's a scoring chance. McClair's through, but the ball bobbles at the last second and slice, the chance has gone. Normally things like

Filling up nicely, about two hours before kick-off

that are greeted with derision, but on this night it was applauded, whistled and cheered – even a throw-in or a half chance was backed up 110% by United's fanatical following.

All around you could see fans in fancy dress giving it some wellie for the cause. Laurel and Hardy, Lucifer and the She Devil, King Kong, Father Christmas, Mrs Thatcher, Quasimodo, Prince Charles and many others were all there. I never knew we had so many celebrity supporters. Sealey had a bandage now – could it hold out? Sparky was like a raging bull, Barcelona had a Dutchman of their own – Koemans – and we all know of his fierce free kicks.

Robson, McClair and Ince covered every blade of grass, Sharpey was exactly that, another 19 year old in a European final – remember Kiddo? Bruce and Pallister took care of Salinas and Goicochea and I've never seen Adolf, err (Phelan), play so well. That lad's taken some stick and so has Sunbed (Blackmore) but this night they were both heroes. And Denis Irwin's barmy army were making all the noise necessary for the quiet Irishman.

When Mark Hughes followed up one of Steve Bruce's now customary headers, we all went mental as the ball was picked out of the net. But when the Welshman skipped over the Spanish goalie, I thought: No he's left it too late, it's too wide, surely, wallop, like an Exocet missile into the net, with Barcelona defenders sliding in hopelessly on their backsides.

With only minutes left Laudrup must have thought his name would be on the score sheet until Clayton came to the rescue to kick the ball away from what would have been a certain goal. But it didn't matter, the ref blew the whistle. Steve Bruce leapt on Pallister's back, Robbo and Chocky did great impressions of sinking a few pints, and Les Sealey, limping with a bandaged knee, collapsed spread-eagled on the ground. The 35,000-plus Manchester United supporters were in a state of mass hysteria leaping around like demented frogs on the first day of Spring. It goes without saying we celebrated well into the night amid scenes I will never forget – pure magic.

Manchester United's switchboard is constantly engaged as most of us have found out. No wonder: they have fans ringing in all the way from Australia before kick off, at half time and after the final whistle, wanting to know the team changes, the scorers and the results. New York, Rio, Copenhagen – you name it they're on the blower asking questions about anything from the car Bryan Robson drives (a black Merc sports) to the type of music Ryan Giggs likes (soul).

The ticket office at Old Trafford boasts members of a 130-odd years old because their season tickets have been handed down from generation to generation. Well I'm heading for middle age and though I hope to see many more championship teams and cup winners, when my kids grow up, they too will join the elite members who profess to be twice as old as the oldest Chelsea pensioner, perpetuating the now legendary Red Army.

It has among its ranks such people as Ian 'Lovejoy' McShane, Mick Hucknell, Rod Stewart, Mike Atherton, Linford Christie, Ronald Biggs, Ulreka Jonsson, Michael 'Kevin' Le Vell from Coronation Street, groups like Take That, New Order, Deep Purple and Iron Maiden. Jack Smethurst, Robert Powell, Terry Christian, Richard 'Victor Meldrew' Wilson, George Roper, Jocky Wilson, honorary members, Pavarotti, the Serb manager of the USA soccer team, and the son of the president of the IOC (International Olympic Committee) Juan Sameranche, Alex Higgins, Lonnie Donegan, Eamon Holmes, Gary Davies, Mike Sweeney, Andie Craine, Terry Hall, Angus Deayton, The Grumbleweeds, Norman Collier, Jimmy Cricket, Roy Walker, The Spinners, Christopher "Cracker" Eccleston and many others.

5

HERE COMES MY NINETEENTH NERVOUS BREAKDOWN

Do you know what it feels like to be so close to something, but just can't touch it, so close you can smell it, the sensations that run through your mind in anticipation of what might be? Well we do. Manchester United supporters more than any other in the league know exactly how that feels. We've been this close on many occasions these last 26 years to the Holy Grail, the championship.

And to say it hurts, to miss out in '92, is an understatement to say the least. Of course it did, but before some out there wring their hands with glee, let us tell you that in the season, not only did we handsomely beat our rivals in both cup competitions, we won games by four, five and six goals, played in Europe yet again, went to Wembley and won three trophies.

So, all in all, it eased the pain a little, because we knew and the whole country knew, that the best team lost on this occasion. It does not come easy, trying to be magnanimous in defeat. We had to hold up our hands and say Leeds were the champions after the 42 games, but no one will ever convince me or any other Reds fan that they weren't as surprised as us and the rest of the nation to be crowned champions at the end of the day.

After the 1967 championship United had quite a few close calls in regaining the Grail. Just 12 months later, in May '68, we were runners up in the league (Nervous Breakdown number 1) but we had another little matter to deal with at the time – down the motorway in London beating Benfica for the European Cup.

A.C. Milan semi '69 – unfortunately some of the players were coming to the end of their career when others were just peaking and we didn't have the right mix (2). Sir Matt had finally found his own personal Grail and decided he'd done all he needed to achieve everything in British and European football. The two things I remember about 1969 was that Neil Armstrong landed on the moon and Sir Matt decided to retire (3). A few managers came and went, some virtually unnoticed and others despatched before he could even settle in and swivel round a couple of times in the "big boss" chair.

Relegation loomed and along came The Doc, Tommy Docherty. He nearly plugged the hole but between Birmingham's big toe and Denis Law's heel they pulled the plug and we swirled down the hole and into the 2nd division (4). A glimmer of what it felt like to actually get your hands on the Holy Grail came along when we found the lid, in the shape of the 2nd division championship in '75 and we all thought, United are back, United are back. Then it happened ... the '76 Southampton Cup Final (5).

Well we may not have won the league in our first year back, but we put the willies up a few people by being front runners for a couple of years. At one point United were 10 points clear but with a trip to Anfield and West Ham ahead. For some reason the Doc put a young fella called Paddy Roache in goal and he literally got crucified, by the fans and on the field. By this time I think I was into the sixth of my nineteen nervous breakdowns.

The Stretford End was still buoyant. The Scoreboard and Paddock were a mass of red, white and tartan with Doc's Red Army marching back to Wembley again, stopping Liverpool's treble hopes in the Queen's Silver Jubilee year and then during the summer of '77, wham, nightmare number 7, the Doc had gone.

In came another quiet man, but a hard man boxer by all accounts – a good coach with a fine reputation. But Manchester United is not just any club – it seemed to overawe the man and he didn't seem to enjoy the media attention particularly. The style of football he created was not, as they say, United football, and not for the first time the manager felt the wrath of the dissatisfied customers. Seven straight wins and an FA Cup Final place still didn't save his bacon.

And oh what a Cup Final. Hard hitting, midfield generals on both sides made it difficult to open up opportunities and we found ourselves 2-0 down with only four minutes to go. Then a goal from the big Scot Gordon McQueen and an absolute beauty from Super Sam McIlroy, the last of the Busby Babes, sent us all into raptures including Dracula, big Joe, Joe, Joe Jordan. He leapt about five feet in the air, I'm sure, well higher than Skip to my Lou anyway.

Thirty Seconds in Football is an Eternity

With only seconds left, Martin Buchan only had to say to the lads: "Calm down, take your time going back to the centre circle and don't let anything get past you", but Liam Brady was having none of that. A quick restart while I and thousands of others were still flat on our backs celebrating in the isle of Wembley's H block terrace and along came number 8 in my calculations, in the guise of Alan Sunderland. Not again I thought. The Southampton final was bad enough, but this just for the sake of a few calming words and someone, anyone to stall the game for 30 seconds. But as you'll see later 30 seconds is an eternity in football terms.

United were in Europe again in '82/'83 and a trip to Valencia was on the drawing board. A last-minute decision and off we went, no ticket, no flights, just cross the channel, avoid the champagne region of France or we'll never get there and it's just down the road from Barca – it'll be a doddle, oh yeah!

Passepartout, my loyal companion, forgot to mention the biggest race of the year in France – the Arc de Triomphe – was on, and all the roads, trains, planes and bleedin' coaches were packed and fully booked for three days solid. On our way we met about 200 Celtic fans heading for Ajax in Amsterdam. They were knocking back half pint glasses full of Pernod with a dash of lemonade to give it a wee kick – we stuck to our cans of Boddies in the rucksack.

Across the Channel and we hit Paris. A night out on the tiles – great, viva la France and all that – we had two days left to get there. After a night out in the city where Leeds nearly had their finest hour we woke up to car horns blaring all around the Arc – about four lanes and eight access roads to the most chaotic roundabout in the world.

We made it across town to the bus depot but to cut a long story short the only coaches available out of Paris were to Madrid – nowhere near the South east coast that we wanted. Because of the gee gees there was nothing available unless you booked three days in advance. We knew United didn't want fans to make their own way into Europe but this was ridiculous. We rushed across town on the underground – no trains to our destinations, just to Nice, at that time of day. The French can be so bloody snotty when they're in a rush, not very helpful like we Mancunians in Piccadilly Gardens at home.

So a few beers and time out to reflect the situation. It was getting late with only a day left to get to Spain. It seemed like millions of Parisians were trying to get home after the day's race meetings. A few more beers and a chat with two blonde Aussie beauties going to Earls Court back-packing across Europe, a few more beers, and Passepartout and I decided. I bet Filius Fogg and Michael Palin never had these connection troubles. Well maybe they did, but money was no object to them. We had the money, we just couldn't find a way out South of Paris, so a few more (hic) beers and it was off back to Blighty – number 9. But the year was not a total wash out – we went on to win the FA Cup and ended up third in the championship race and City went down thanks to Luton.

Nine down, ten to go

A year later we finished fourth which wasn't too bad, and this time we were prepared for another go at Europe. That season we saw Platini, Maradona and Rossi to name but a few, while City were having day trips to Swansea and Brighton and the like. Barcelona were behind us and the semis were looming and it was off to Turin. We were so confident we'd get to the final in Switzerland.

We had planned to borrow my mate's Mercedes estate car, contacted the Camping Resort for a chalet, drawn the route and even divided out the cost between four of us – petrol money, beer money, cost for two nights' stay, more beer money, tickets, ferry, oh and more beer money, just to be on the safe side.

All was well at the game. We were flanked by the carabiniere, deafened by the booming fireworks, but high up in the stand among all the din the Italians' hearts weren't in it. "Norman, Norman", we cried as the Irishman smashed the ball into the net after coming on as sub – 1-1 and United started to believe they could do it. Then with just 50 seconds of the game left Juventus got a free kick near the penalty area. Bailey didn't stand a chance and bang it was all over – the time 89 minutes and 30 seconds. I didn't cheer for Rossi this time I can tell you. I just wanted to walk over the border and spend the two days in the Swiss chalet in a dark cupboard somewhere. My 10th nervous breakdown you must agree, was particularly cruel.

Kevin Moran's sending off in '85 was really nerve racking and hearing and seeing on TV the Bradford fire was too (11). A very sad day. A fresh start in the '86 season saw United nearly break a record with 10 wins on the trot and 15 unbeaten, but we fell at the gate again, finishing 4th and that was the end of Big Ron (12).

A couple of years passed when we finished runners up in '88 (13) and got robbed by Forest in the Cup (14). Don't get me wrong, it wasn't always doom and gloom, we won trophies left right and centre, but the Holy Grail had eluded us all these years, and we were wondering just what United had to do to find it.

Pavarotti puts his weight behind United!

We heard the team were training with the SAS. The Prime Minster was on TV, in the Houses of Parliament, congratulating us on our victory in Rotterdam, and the exemplary conduct of our supporters – the first in a European final since English clubs were allowed back into Europe. The night the team toured the city, Pavarotti donned a United scarf and hat and sang in the G-Mex centre.

The '92 season got under way with a 16-game unbeaten run in the league and cup, a hiccup against Atletico Madrid and Sheffield Wednesday, and another 12 games unbeaten. Top of the table past Christmas and only one league game lost, 2-3 away from home. 4-0, 5-0 and 6-3 victories on the way, then dong went the bells of Big Ben. In came the New Year and January the 1st – the 1-4 defeat by QPR. Rumour has it the boys were celebrating

The Terminator, Hughesie, and his second spectacular goal in the '91 ECWC Final against Barcelona in Rotterdam

The

End

of an

era!

in the Midland Hotel just a little longer than club rules allow.

I'm sure Fergie did right by the club, but on hearing "the bells" did someone spike his orange juice while he sang Auld Lang Syne? The two things we fans just don't understand are the manager's team choices and substitutions. Queens Park Rangers first ever win at OT definitely gave me breakdown number 15.

Just a week later, United met Leeds for the third time that season. After a couple of 1-1 draws in the league it was away in the League Cup this time – fate had drawn the two top-placed clubs in the country together in the FA Cup also within a week of each other. And after the QPR fiasco, surely we couldn't play that badly again, could we? Of course not. United came out 3-1 winners with one of them being an absolute blast-from-the-past Bobby Charlton-type rocket from Clayton Sunbed Blackmore, immediately forgiven for his part in the stinker on New Year's Day.

A second bite at the cherry for Leeds came in the FA Cup tie where the home fans were giving Hughesie some stick. McClair got Giggs free on the wing and just before half time Mark Hughes got a brilliant cross and with three Leeds defenders after him went Whollop 'stitch that', and headed into the net in the 44th minute from a yard or two out, right in front of the home supporters' favourite terrace. He said later: "At that point, I even enjoyed the abuse" and that victory meant United had only lost one out of 13 games played at Elland Road – unlucky for some eh!

Lady Luck was not on our side in the next round of the FA Cup – a 2-2 draw against Southampton meant United went out on penalties, but not before Robbo had scored a legitimate goal which was definitely over the line. But the ref disallowed it and we were out of the cup (16). We'd had some ups and downs in the previous seasons, but this one was a stormer.

A new Best?

A month after the Saints defeat, two great games

The new Stretford End, like the Phoenix risen from the ashes

The genius George Best at work and play,
delighting a packed Stretford End in the sixties.
(By permission: Eastern Counties Newspapers)

were saying "you've had it now". I can tell you those Boro boys put up a hell of a fight in this semi final second leg. 1-1 at full time, it went into extra time, and, as many times before, the Stretford End just turned up the volume and the whole stadium responded. Giggsy, the so-called new George Best, did his stuff and rose to the occasion with a goal.

Besty is my all-time hero but when young Giggs shimmies one way and the defender goes the other, and he puts them off balance or scores a classic goal from an unbelievable angle, just for that split second, as his skinny frame flaps around in that baggy shirt, you'd swear the genial Irishman was back on the field. In the opinion of many fans his crossing is his only weakness, but apart from that this lad has everything. If he carries on the way he has started, he won't need a GB tag, he'll be the number one and the many new Fergie fledglings will want to emulate him. Anyway the final score was 2-1 to United and we were off to Wembley again.

Nice football, shame about the game

A lot of people said the League Cup Final between United and Forest was a good clean advert for professional football. It wasn't the most exciting match, but in a tactical and clinically footballing sense it was a good game with Chocky McClair getting the winner, and it was that final that really started off United's run of a ridiculous five games in 10 days. Too many draws and a revenge result for losing the cup to Forest was just too much for any team especially when that team had freed its rivals from both cups some three months earlier.

Oh! and talking of knocking out rivals from both cups, the City fans went awfully quiet at work after Middlesborough knocked them out of both cups. Despite what Liverpool fans were chanting at Anfield, we didn't actually lose the title on the Mersey like they did against Arsenal. A lot of fans feel it actually started with the draw at Luton which United couldn't really afford (17). That's when I started with the doubt that it may not just be our year, again.

And to see West Ham, who were already doomed, play like demons was just unbelievable. To see Sheffield self-destruct at home against Leeds was it for me. The goals that Leeds got and

Sheffield gave away were just too much to bear – before United had even touched the ball against the Merseysiders. But we still sang our hearts out for the lads even in defeat. "Over and Over, we will follow you", the Red Army sang – guts and character, the players and fans never gave up their loyalty right up to the final whistle. Definitely seeing the Sheffield game on TV that evening was number 18.

George Best, Superstar

George Best was one of the world's first footballing superstars. Okay – Stanley Matthews, Tom Finney, Duncan Edwards, Puskas, John Charles, Charlie Tulley, Dixie Deans and many others were all footballing stars long before GB came along, but none of them, including Charlton, Pele and Beckenbauer, had the kind of pop star, film star following that the Irish imp had.

In the swinging '60s, between them Best, Law and Charlton had everything a team's line up needed, but GB did things with a ball on that field that, as far as I can remember, no one could even get close to emulating. He could add 10,000 spectators on an away gate all by himself, and on many occasions more than 10,000 were locked out at Old Trafford in the '60s and '70s.

There are those in the world of sport who have since written that GB threw it all away, that it was a waste of natural talent. Other fans ridicule the man, causing many a heated argument from those of us who actually saw him play in the flesh.

I was privileged to see Georgie on many occasions, having great games and stinkers. But as the saying goes: It is better to have loved and lost than never to have loved at all and all those fans who didn't see GB play are, I am afraid, "loveless" – that is until now. Managers say a player like GB only comes along once in a lifetime. Well someone up there must be a Manchester United fan because we have been sent Ryan Giggs!

When I hear people making disparaging remarks about Georgie, I think of the time I met him. I was at home listening to the radio when the DJ said that George Best was in town signing his new book at a major store in the Arndale. It was a spur of the moment thing – I rushed to find my camera had only two frames left on the reel. So I grabbed it and a pen and a bit of paper hoping to get his autograph. I went to one of Manchester's top hotels and asked the receptionist whether

top hotels and asked the receptionist whether George had checked out yet, kidding on that I knew him personally and taking a wild guess that this was the hotel he'd chosen.

Bingo, I'd guessed right. The young lady said he had checked out but he was just coming down the elevator. Ping, went the lift doors behind me in the lobby. My heart missed a beat as I turned round in anticipation and out stepped . . . a gorgeous blonde. Normally this sight would attract my full, undivided attention, but on this occasion I just dismissed her entrance and sat patiently on a comfy leather chair with a direct view of the lifts.

As I sat wondering what I would say to my hero and how he would react when approached, I heard the sound of well healed shoes heading towards me. As I glanced up, the gorgeous blonde was none other than his wife Angie Best who placed his book and the daily papers on the table in front of us. I introduced myself and asked if she would ask George for his autograph on my behalf and she said: "Of course, and would you like a photo?", picking up my camera.

Suddenly the lift doors pinged again and my hero appeared, in a dusky pink sweater and black patterned slacks. He came over and his wife introduced us. George looked great – slim, clean shaven and he had a genuine handshake for a loyal Stretford Ender. A quick chat and a photo or two and he had to go off to the Arndale for his sitting. Angie spoke with him for a moment then came over to me with my camera and as she handed it over she placed some money in my hand and I said: "I can't take that". She said: "Go on, you can get the book and a cab home with it. I won't miss it and George won't mind". George asked: "See you down there?" You what? – wild horses couldn't drag me away.

When I arrived at the store, hundreds of Reds were packing in the entrances. I thought I'd never get to the front and just as I tried to get in among the throng from another angle the man arrived, escorted through the excited crowd by security, towards the waiting press photographers. All of a sudden he and his wife saw me struggling to get through and Angie beckoned me to the front. The fans turned as if to say: "Who's he, and how come he knows them?" George said: "Hello again, glad to see you made it", and I got the very first book, the only one signed by my hero and his beautiful and charming wife Angie.

I didn't have to pay for it either. I did get a cab home and that night I raised a glass or two and toasted Georgie Best and his wife for their kindness and generosity. So don't believe everything you hear about the hell-raising bearded, womanising character the media write about, for I will always remember him as a footballing genius with a genuine fondness for his loyal fans.

Running off the rails there a little, let's get back to the end of the 1992 season and my final breakdown.

Great Sportmanship

The last match of the '92 season was against Spurs. All the Reds present in that most hallowed of terracing conducted themselves impeccably and were a credit to the many generations who had stood there before them, singing for our gallant heroes in the red shirts of Manchester United, with great sportsmanship.

I know that hasn't always been the case over the years, but on this day that is the most appropriate word I can use, as the rest of the ground's fans applauded us and the great fight our team had put up throughout the season. A 3-1 victory was the least the boys could do to repay our loyalty and as the Stret was to be demolished I'm sure they didn't want to go out on a whimper.

Brian McClair who scored first was, in my opinion, one of United's best buys in the last 10 years. Fergie admits he is forever playing him out of position, but does Brain complain or whinge? No, he just gets on with his job – he scores goals. Not as many as when he was up front, but just think, without his goals we wouldn't have got to Rotterdam or to a few Wembley finals either. Okay, he's missed a few penalties, but at least he had the bottle to go up and take them, and he's the most consistent player in the team. He never gets injured and plays well in any position and defends when needed. All in all, Chocky is first on our pub team sheet if not always Fergie's.

Hughesie, who got the other two goals, has netted more since Eric arrived. He's scored some absolute corkers for us over the years, especially the ones against Liverpool in the '85 semi at Maine Road, the 'King' type scissor kick spectacular in the Derby – the one our neighbours are always raving about and, of course, his second in Holland against the mighty Barca. Hughesie's a Red to the core.

This could be the last time . . .

There used to be a little man who stood on Warwick Road bridge in a bowler hat and with a placard with "The end is nigh!" on it. Well, for the Stretford End it was a bit nigh-er than ever this day, as we applauded a goal scored by an opposing player – Gary Lineker – in his last game at Old Trafford before he went to Japan.

The 86th minute goal was given a great reception from the Stretford Enders – a very rare sight indeed, and it brought this response later. "What a way to go. I've never before had a reception like that from opposing supporters, that Stretford End is something else. It was very touching and is something I will always remember". Nice one Gary. As the whistle went, I was not ashamed to shed a tear and neither were thousands of others that day.

The songs were being sung – "We'll support you ever more" echoing down the tunnel and staircases. We just aimed for the exit and I just turned for one last look – a panoramic view, the roof, pigeons coming in to land, the cartons, tickets, papers blowing across the left side, the rest of the stadium looking resplendent. Just a few seconds, that's all it was, then a draught came and swept across my face and I thought how many souls have swept through here feeling what I'm feeling now.

This is my club, this is my Stretford End. It goes without saying, that that moment was unbearable. The men in white coats from Prestwich funny farm mistook me for one of their patients, but after I remonstrated they let me go home to have my 19th nervous breakdown in peace.

The Holy Grail just eluded us yet again, but we know now that it was just a matter of a short summer and the crusades would be over. August couldn't come quick enough, we had it in our sights, so close we could smell it. Oh yes, we know what it's like to miss out alright, and hopefully now you've read this, so do you.

6

ALWAYS LOOK ON THE BRIGHT SIDE

Do you remember the good old days when you could have a laugh and a joke with your fellow supporters and still shake hands after you've taken the pickle out of each other's teams? No? Well, I do. We all used to have a laugh about Franny Lee being a womble or Bobby Charlton's slap head and his needing a walking stick, or Mike Summerbee's nose or Georgie Best's frilly shorts, even Steptoe Stepney, Snapper Stiles and dubious remarks about Colin Bell and Mike Doyle. They were all in the best possible taste.

But then, as with most of today's new wave comedians, things turned sour – it wasn't funny unless you were being sarcastic or downright obnoxious. It wasn't worth the trouble it caused to mix with other fans on away trips and, unfortunately, it developed from there. We now have the situation where we have mass segregation inside and outside most of our major stadiums, though, as you've probably noticed, there has been an improvement in recent years.

There used to be some Reds from Chadderton near Oldham who did impressions like the Grumbleweeds on the football specials (trains) and one lad who we saw every other away game was brilliant at Norman Wisdom and Bernard Cribbins. He used to have us in stitches. Before the beer ban on the trains, we used to get tickets off Dave Smith the supporters' club chairman from the back of a van outside Piccadilly or Victoria stations. Then we'd board the train and scramble for a carriage with a card table or an individual carriage where we could tie the door shut with a scarf if we were lucky enough to cop off with some girls out for a good time with the lads.

Card schools used to pay for your beers and match programme, if you got a good hand or two. Football cards and lottery tickets were flowing as fast as the vodka and cokes disguised in pop bottles and people paid fortunes to anyone who had a spare fag, buttie or the most precious, a can of beer or juice on the way home because we would sing ourselves hoarse at the game. But more often than not the camaraderie was good and they were freely handed over.

Get a Life

A good sing song and a crack or two at station masters at various stoppages up and down the country, and a good day out was had by all. I think most fans will recognise that, not just United fans. But if you take umbridge at any of these jokes think on: you'll see a lot worse in your own personal club's fanzines or newsletters. So get a life, better still get a sense of humour because it's all harmless fun.

Terrace humour is very spontaneous and unique to football and the working classes. At times it seems chauvinistic and crude but that's because it is still one of the few male dominated bastions left where the lads can still let their hair down and enjoy a good shout at the referee, linesman and players. As long as you don't go over the top and get arrested or asked to leave the ground, it is still a good Saturday afternoon's entertainment.

So here is a peep at the brighter side of football: some very corny jokes, some naughty but nice cartoons and stories from both sides, Blue and Red. The popular fanzines do have their brighter side and the barra boys (street vendors) outside the grounds do have some very original and amusing T-shirts. The inflatables may have all but gone but it seems, at last, the fans themselves are trying to put a bit of fun back into football, even if it is sometimes a bit near the knuckle.

Go to sleep. The Cup Final isn't until two weeks on Saturday.

I don't care who's playing today . . . get it off!

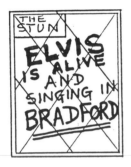

I don't believe it....

I don't believe it

.... I don't ...mmm?

How do you save money at Wembley? ...support Manchester City because they never get there ..ooh!

Moses parted the waves, but then Giggsy surfed on them!

First Mars Mission

Courtesy of Red Issue

Courtesy of Red Issue

FOOTY FUN TOP 20

TITLE	ARTIST	REQUESTED FOR
20 MY WAY	(FRANK SINATRA)	A FERGUSON
19 MONEY TALKS	(AC/DC)	A S HEARER
18 LAST MINUTE MIRACLE	(THE SHIRRELLS)	S BRUCE
17 I STARTED SOMETHING I COULDN'T FINISH	(THE SMITHS)	I W RIGHT
16 FROM RUSSIA WITH LOVE	(MATT MUNRO)	A KANCHELSKIS
15 ARE YOU READY TO BE HEARTBROKEN	(SANDY SHAW)	K K EEGAN
14 TOO GOOD TO BE FORGOTTEN	(AMAZULU)	B McCLAIR
13 LIVING IN ANOTHER WORLD	(TALK TALK)	M C ITYFANS
12 NICE LEGS SHAME ABOUT THE FACE	(MONKS)	N M CNAB
11 HEAVEN MUST HAVE SENT YOU	(THE ELGINS)	R GIGGS
10 SWEET DREAMS ARE MADE OF THIS	(EURYTHMICS)	R EDARMY
9 BORN TO BE WILD	(STEPPENWOLF)	M HUGHES
8 DON'T BELIEVE THE HYPE	(PUBLIC ENEMY)	V JONES
7 ANOTHER ONE BITES THE DUST	(QUEEN)	P INCE
6 IT'S A DIRTY JOB BUT SOMEONES GOTTA DO IT	(BONNY TYLER)	G S OUMESS
5 SHOULD I STAY OR SHOULD I GO	(THE CLASH)	E CANTONA
4 DANCIN MACHINE	(JACKSON 5)	L SHARPE
3 REMEMBER YOUR A WOMBLE	(THE WOMBLES)	F LEE
2 WHO'S SORRY NOW	(CONNIE FRANCIS)	H W ILKINSON

AND AT NUMBER ONE FOR A RECORD 17 YEARS ...... ITS

1 SAD SWEET DREAMER (SWEET SENSATION) P S WALES

BUBBLING UNDER

ONE'S TO WATCH

MAMA WERE ALL CRAZY NOW	(SLADE)	K STAND
I AM KING	(JIMMY CLIFFE)	D LAW
I MISSED AGAIN	(PHIL COLLINS)	I R USH
POETRY IN MOTION	(JOHNNY TILLOTSON)	G BEST
I CAN'T STAND UP FOR FALLING DOWN	(ELVIS COSTELLO)	J B ARNES
STARS SHINE IN YOUR EYES	(RONNIE HILTON)	SIR MATT
ROCKET MAN	(ELTON JOHN)	B CHARLTON
DO YOU FEEL LIKE WE DO	(PETER FRAMPTON)	EXECUTIVE CLUB CLASS
LIFE WON'T EVER BE THE SAME	(HADDAWAY)	STRETFORD END
DIRTY DEEDS DONE DIRT CHEAP	(AC/DC)	M D OYLE
TELL ME WHY I DON'T LIKE MONDAYS	(BOOMTOWN RATS)	THE DOC
PRIDE	(U2)	B ROBSON

Reproduced by permission: *Manchester Evening News*

Terry Waite's first words when he was freed were... has Ian Rush scored against United yet?

What's the difference between Leeds and a tea bag?
... the tea bag stays longer in the cup
- Boom, Boom!

Some of the Fun T-Shirts the "barra boys" sell outside O.T.

...and a couple you might see around town.

MAJOR BOO-BOOs OF THE 20th CENTURY:

"It doesn't matter what running shoes Jessie Owens wears, I'm sure he won't beat our boys."
- Adolf Hitler 1938.

"Listen Shilts: don't worry about Maradona on crosses - he'll never reach those high balls"
- Bobby Robson 1986.

"Eric, me flower, I dorn't think tha' goin' to git thang o' tha Queen's English in training sessions. How dust tha fancy a moove ta Manchester?"
"Oui"
"Fust left darn corridor, and hurry up."
- H. Wilkinson, 1992.

Subbuteo were going to bring out a new Manchester City set of players, but they gave up because none of them would go in the box.

Jesus Saves but Georgie Best always netted the rebound!

Isn't it marvellous the support we have when 16,000 turn up to watch UTD on closed circuit TV? ...City tried it - their fans sat there for two minutes then turned over to watch the film on the other side
- Boom, Boom!

Noddy said to Big Ears: is that the house that Jack built?
And Big Ears said NO - that's Maine Road,

It's all ours . . .team and club captain, Bryan Robson and Steve Bruce. Campionés 1993!

The last farewell: players applaud the Stretford Enders on the last day of the '92 season

Unforgettable, that's what you are: Alex Ferguson and Sir Matt Busby with even more silverware for the trophy cabinet

FROM ROCHDALE TO RIO
THE UNITED COLOURS

. . . WE WILL FOLLOW YOU
OF MANCHESTER!

The Duncan Edwards stained-glass window at
St Francis' church, Dudley, West Midlands.

7

RED DEVILS, BORN TO RAVE LIKE HELL

When it came to this chapter, I thought: How do you go about writing about fan's allegiances to clubs and freedom of choice without winding them up? No matter who you write about, someone's going to get the hump. So come on lads, play the game, put aside your pet hates and jealousies, it gets in the way of common sense and fair play. Credit where credit is due and all that. Then I thought: If they've read this far into the book they'll see I'm a football supporter who appreciates everyone's right to support any club they wish.

I may not agree with their choice of club but everyone's entitled to pledge allegiance to one, two or half a dozen clubs if they want to. I obviously try to encourage everyone I meet to support Manchester United, but if they choose Wycombe Wanderers, that's fine too. Football needs all the fans it can get before it loses a whole generation – because their parents have had enough of the bovver – to some other pastime.

The sooner we fans start talking and mixing together again as we used to the better. As a supporter it's been hard to ignore the bad side of soccer. Without dwelling on it too much, we all know that football has had its fair share of troubles. In the '60s some clubs had followers like Rockers-only or Mods-only gangs. Then came the first wave of skinheads in the late '60s and early '70s, followed by the boot boys dressed in white butcher's coats covered in graffiti or Clockwork Orange clones. The '80s saw certain followers in various guises: new wave punk skins, firms, casuals, intercity crews – the list is probably endless.

As teenagers we were all a little hot headed and rebellious and did things we later regretted, but as we grow older most of us settle down, either that or end up a cross between Victor Meldrew and Hannibal Lecter. I mean, no decent fans like to see things like the Burnden Park and Ibrox disasters, the Bradford fire, Heysell or Hillsborough and the like. United fans don't need reminding that in our history our own followers have had their fair share of rumbles, a lot of which I'm sure could have been avoided except for taunts from certain quarters about our own club's misfortunes.

Thankfully things seemed to have calmed down in the '90s and have turned a little brighter with the emergence of a brief craze for inflatables and a tendency for a lot of fans to get kitted out in fancy dress for the last match of the season and on foreign tours. Now it's painted faces and ravers out for a good time.

If you are a genuine fan, a United fan or not, you'll have probably noticed more and more fans mixing out and around the stadiums, home and away, wearing their colours without being subjected to all sorts of abuse from opposing supporters. Let's not get complacent, there are still one or two sets of fans that just don't mix, so it's going to take time.

True Loyalty

I eat, sleep and breathe Manchester United. I drive my family and workmates absolutely mad. Hardly a day goes by when they're not in my thoughts and, although I have a soft spot for the Glasgow club in the green and white hoops, let no one question my loyalty to the club that's not only tattooed on my arm, but engraved on my heart and will be lovingly cherished till the day I die.

So if you like the Villa, Oldham or Toy Town FC that's okay. We all watch each other's teams on TV and whether we want one team to win or the other it's the game that counts. We all have mates who are opposing fans, but that doesn't make us go out and kick seven bells out of each other every other weekend. We just give each other some friendly stick and a bit of leg pulling, and the next week it will be Tom, Dick or Harriet's turn whoever wins or loses. If we can go

to work and the pub with these people, why not the match?

The trouble is, the media especially don't print enough good stories about football fans who actually do good deeds – our image, particularly in the middle and upper classes, is that we're all branded hooligans. TV and the national press could start to improve that image by doing more articles on things like the Reds who saved someone in the Manchester Ship Canal or the family who were rescued from a house fire by five United fans in May 1992.

Below: some favourite United reviews. My, how things have changed!

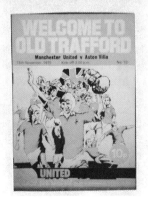

The charities we help every other week at OT, more like the great reports that came back from Rotterdam and the championship celebrations, would help to redress the balance. And the club's programme letter page used to inform us of Reds who had helped and befriended our own and away fans broken down on the motorway in the pouring rain, or had done some commendable deed which had helped to dismantle the barriers that we all as fans have built up over the years. For me, the sooner the club reinstate the programme letter page (warts and all) the better.

I know this is the supporters' view of what it's like to follow United, but wherever I go on my travels there's one question that keeps cropping up: "What's all this United/Celtic, United/Rangers stuff, what's the connection?" To be quite honest I can't really tell you, apart from some time in the late '60s early '70s different sides of the Stretford End used to chant "Celtic, Rangers, Celtic, Rangers" at half time when the results were put up on the scoreboard or announced on the tannoy.

But wait a minute! A recent one (bottom right) bears an uncanny resemblance to an old fourpenny one!

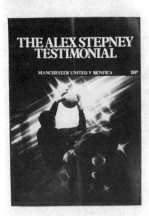

I don't think United have any political or religious affiliations these days – maybe in the past. It's all big business now and even those other old taboos like black players and Spurs Jewish connections are all old hat. Football is a cosmopolitan world game now, and there's no room for all that, especially when fans are trying to turn a cease fire into permanent friendly rivalry.

United have had numerous internationals at OT, including matches against Russians, Italians, Danes, Yugoslavians, South Africans, Northern and Southern Irish, Scots and Welsh. Tommy Docherty once said if he found a player from Mars with pink and green spots and he was good enough, he'd sign him. United have supporters and club branches all over the British isles from Lands End to John o' Groats, from Norwich to Galway and hundreds of branches all over the world.

Anyway how many clubs' fans have you seen with Arsenal/Celtic, Chelsea/Rangers, Villa/Celtic and Blackburn/Rangers split ski hats and scarfs? Why should United and City be any different? United have Celtic and Rangers split with Man U's colours so some reds like Celtic and some Rangers. But does it really matter? All we know is someone is making a fortune out of woolly hats! Why are they only split with Celtic or Rangers – why not City and Real Madrid or United and Juventus? We've no idea.

After asking hundreds of Reds, why they think United get on well with Celtic, they said it's because they've had quite a few testimonials and friendlies against the Glasgow club for players such as Bobby Charlton, Jimmy Johnstone, Lou Macari, Roy Aitkin, Bryan Robson and others. These games had terrific atmospheres with very little or no trouble at all. They were what football is supposed to be all about – having a good time no matter which club we are playing or which fans we're mixing with!

Fanzines

In the interests of research for this book, I have been given a dozen or so Red and Blue fanzines to browse through to get genned up on what the young and trendy are all going mad to collect these days. City's were more of a journalistic serious type of reporting, whereas United's were a mixture – full colour covers, adverts, serious articles concerning fans, comic strip cartoons, jokes and letter pages. I did wonder how they get away with half the things they put – they're a bit near the knuckle. They made Bernard Manning's jokes fit for Blue Peter.

Now I'm as broad-minded as the next fan. Any Blue noses (City fans) or Red rags (United fans) jokes about 5-1, or Robbo and Fergie or Colin Bell and Howard Kendal, City's lack of silverware and us blowing the title are fair game but I was disappointed with one article, about Munich. After having a good chuckle about both fanzines' terrace humour, the editors could have printed the piece in a less sadistic fashion.

It seems a sad reflection of just how much they are constantly preoccupied with what United are doing, instead of trying to get behind their own team, and portraying a more positive image, by getting our club's supporters back to some sort of normality and sporting rivalry instead of prolonging ill feeling. The death of any fan, player or sports journalist is not a subject to laugh about, and any fans gloating over such a thing, when one of their own, Frank Swift, was also tragically taken from the world of sport, don't deserve to call themselves fans of football.

That's the first and last time the disaster will be mentioned in this book.

Now let's look at the brighter side of football supporters. Over the years United fans have had some absolutely stonking celebrations. Part of all the fun has been meeting fellow Reds from all four corners of the globe, some well known, some unknown. Some I only met one day and I've never seen since while others I met one day and have become lifelong friends as well as blood brothers, if only in spirit. Young and old, black and white, yellow or martian, we all have one thing in common – the love of Manchester United Football Club.

We've tried to give you the feel of the spirit of the fans and you'll notice a lot of changes in the fan's styles, fashions, haircuts and we've tried to be honest in our comments on all supporters. If any of our Blue friends are a bit miffed about offending articles just think how United fans feel when they do the offending. Enough is enough, we should start acting more civilised towards each other, have a good chin wag about the game . . . and then take the mickey out of each other. Having said all that, I still made damn sure the wife didn't follow City before I married her.

8

SIMPLY READ:
FANS' QUESTIONNAIRE

A questionnaire survey was put to a cross section of supporters from all areas of the ground between August and September of 1993. Most of the fans lived within a 15-mile radius of the stadium and their ages ranged from 12 to 52. Here are the most popular answers, but please note: **these views are those of the fans and not necessarily those of the author or contributors:**

Why did you pick UTD as your team?

Family tradition, all the family are reds.

Family all reds – why spoil a good thing?

As Tina says, "They're simply the best".

My grandad started the ball rolling, now the whole family are red barmy.

Because my dad tried to make me kick a funny-shaped ball, I hated it.

God sent me a vision of George Best in the sixties.

Any other favourite team?

United reserves.

Celtic.

Notts Forest.

Sunderland.

Rangers.

Charlton.

What would you ask Martin Edwards?

More members must be allowed access to O.T. after paying their fees, so please enlarge the stadium.

Build another tier above the Stretford End

I'd ask him never to sell Ryan Giggs.

Why can't you build a members' bar so ordinary fans can enjoy the facilities, not just the Club Class?

Why can't you lead the top six clubs to bring down the price of transfer fees?

Football superstitions?

Always take same route to ground, and always wear my UTD badge – every day.

Never place a bet on United, ever.

I never wash my scarf during the season.

Never buy sky-blue jumpers or ties.

Always wear the same shirt until we lose, then change it.

Favourite away fixture?

Liverpool and Everton because they are great games, usually in our favour.

Sheffield Wednesday, as it's a good day out and a great atmosphere.

Leeds – I've never seen us lose there, and they're ever so friendly.

Manchester Derby.

Villa Park, great atmosphere.Newcastle United

Best stadium visited?

New Park, Westhoughton – beats Ibrox to second place.

Highbury.

Villa Park

Athletico Madrid.

Wembley.

Nou Camp, Barcelona.

The new Olympic Stadium in Athens – sunk in the ground for shade from the sun.

Friendliest fans?

Glasgow Celtic.

Newcastle United away in the Black Bull Pub – 1990/91 season.

Sheffield Wednesday, as they wear their colours (unlike some) and mix in their pubs with no trouble.

Nottingham Forest at Rumbelows Cup Final before the game.

Glasgow Rangers (honest!).

Most Norwegian and Scandinavian fans.

Eastern Europeans and Celtic.

Luton and Celtic.

Charlton Athletic

Coventry

How do you spend your time in the summer when there is no football?

Doing the gardening and winding my blue-nosed mate up for 3 months.

Totally bored . . . scuba diving in the Caribbean . . . dreaming of glorious MUFC.

Kicking stones

Funniest thing on the way to a game?

A game of football in a traffic jam on the M6 near the junction with the M1, on our way to the Brighton 1983 F.A. Cup Final reply.

A big grey Glasgow police horse head butted a Rangers fan and bit several others after they chanted, "There's only one Desert Orchid".

Seeing a Chelsea fan stubbing his cigarette out on a police horse's rear end; the shocked horse peed on him and he got arrested.

Seeing United fans wearing plastic beer bellies and Gazza masks outside the Spurs ground. When the Spurs coach went past with the real Gazza on it, he found it funny too.

At an away Wimbledon game there was a minibus full of reds in fancy dress. Two were dressed as Laurel and Hardy and they stood behind two coppers, mimicking their every move with all the reds falling about laughing. The plod never cottoned on.

What would you like changed on TV football?

The BBC should analyse controversial issues such as fixture pile ups, transfer fees, admission prices etc.

For ITV and BBC to win back the contract for Premier League Football from Sky.

More live games on ITV and BBC and a change of celebrities.

Don't put two games on different channels at the same time.

Replace Elton Welsby with a Spitting Image Puppet and get rid of the Sky dizzy dancers.

Favourite (non-United) player/s?

Cole and Sutton

Paul McStay and Le Tissier

Van Basten and, in the past, Pele.

Papin and McCoist.

Ray Wilkins and Nick Barmby.

Greatest moment as a UTD fan?

Winning the European Cup in 1968 and FA Cup in 1977.

So many to choose from, winning the championship watching with a tear in me eye.

Winning the Championship and Rotterdam 1991.

Winning the Championship at Crystal Palace 1993.

E.C.W.E. 1st leg in Poland 3-1 up – absolute magic.

Worst moment?

Seeing Ian Rush score against us at Anfield 1992.

Losing to Southampton in 1976 F.A. Cup Final (definitely an offside goal).

Losing the League title in 1992.

Torpedo Moscow: losing away on penalties a long way from home after being 2-0 up.

Selling Denis Law on a free to City.

Most memorable incident?

On our way to Rotterdam we had a great 100-a-side game of football in the Dover ferryport car park with reds from all over Britain and Ireland – at 5.30 in the morning.

Our 'red army' trudging through Manchester Airport and wearing Russian hats after the game against Torpedo Moscow

Singing my head off as Steve Coppell scored against Leeds in the mid-70s. We walked into Leeds along the railway track to see the smiling faces of the Leeds fans about to wave us off. It brought a tear to my eye, the one I had left after that game.

When United played Ayathanikos in Athens, we had a holiday in Greece. Being good ambassadors, we gave away our United hats and scarves to some guys outside the ground. After the match, we went into a restaurant and the waiters were dressed in United colours - they were the ones we'd met earlier and they all worked at the same restaurant! We chose the restaurant at random from the hundreds in the centre of Athens.

9

GETTING TOO BIG FOR THEIR BOOTS

As they say: "It's a funny old game" but just recently over the last five years or so, various things have been creeping in to spoil the harmony between football and its supporters. For over 100 years things have been fairly amicable – 22 blokes kicking a leather ball up and down a field exciting the fans every time they miraculously got it between the two wooden bits at either end. A few meat pies and bottles of Double Diamond were consumed. Referees' parenthood and eyesight were questioned, a quick pee at half time, a natter and a sing song and everyone went home happy and contented till the following Saturday.

But the fans think the people who run the game are rapidly losing sight of what the beautiful game is all about. First it was the ID card fiasco then the Taylor Report, then Bond schemes, replica kits, price increases and now it's Monday night, Sunday morning, Thursday lunchtime kick offs pampering to the whims of satellite TV companies' ratings wars. Not for one minute do they take into consideration the inconvenience to, or opinions of, the fans, the very people for whom they purport to run this entertainment business.

That's what it is or should be, entertainment. And yes we do realise it's a business, and unfortunately the business is being put before the entertainment. They reckon they can do exactly what they like with the game and we'll follow like lemmings. Okay, we're not fools but the football comes first, the game is everything. We don't need plastic pop up seats or billion dollar prima donnas. True fans get the same buzz watching kids playing with two piles of coats for goal posts as we do watching the Brazilian dream team in a World Cup Final.

Beyond Criticism

Is our club now so big that it's beyond constructive criticism? I really do hope not – it would be a shame. But a lot of the fans think our beloved club is becoming very insular when it comes to the slightest criticism or view of indifference. This book wouldn't be a truly honest reflection of what it's like to follow United, if I only wrote about the good times. If it's okay for the chairman, ex-managers and sports journalists to write about important issues that concern the fans, why can't the fans do likewise?

As I said in the introduction we're not here to dig up dirt. You only have to visit any library to see our club's chequered history and although we'd all like to forget certain events in our lives they shouldn't be swept under the carpet as though they didn't happen. The period I'm talking about was a major crisis for most of the fans in the Stretford End and was only just averted at the 11th hour.

I must stress that this chapter is not a dig at our club, board or chairman personally. If we wanted to be controversial there's plenty to go at: the World in Action programme, the Doc's departure, Maxwell's bid, the Knighton fiasco, Dave Smith's book, Cup Final ticket distribution, the touts, replica kits, price increases and so on. The fans know all about these already and the facts can be read about elsewhere I'm sure. They all affected us, the fans, in some way. None of the above was of the fans' doing, yet we are as much a part of the club as the chairman, directors, manager, players and staff, and like the club we have to live with it.

Whatever affects the club also reflects on the fans. If the club have a bad defeat, the players can retreat to the golf course for peace and sanctuary.

But fans get it in the neck at work, at home off relatives, in the boozer – it's relentless. Fans have long memories and are constantly reminded by others of the club's errors, be it a minor faux pas like requesting blue-nosed worms or a major thing like the Knighton affair. But any fan worth his salt defends the club's honour against all comers. And that's the difference between those who are loyal for love and those there for business and whose loyalty is to whoever has the biggest cheque book.

Very rarely does an opportunity come along when the supporters get their say and now that we have, we're hoping it will be received in the manner in which it is intended – constructive criticism. Football is all about gut feelings, emotions and passion. Our boss Fergie knows that, every manager knows that. How many times have we seen at games and on TV, disagreements in the heat of the moment because a decision or result has gone the other way? Well, the fans are no different.

How many times have you had a row with the wife when she's said: "You love that bloody team more than me"? How many times have you had relatives say: "They don't give a monkeys about you, it's your money they want"? Have you missed family weddings or anniversaries? Well I have. I had my 21st at OT in the first executive suite built and I proposed while having dinner sitting next to the FA Cup.

Okay I don't profess to be United's number one fan, I know plenty worthy of that title. I've probably missed 10 or 12 games in the last 25 years and, now that I'm married with a young family, I may not get to as many away games as I'd like. But I've done my fair share of duty in United Red Army manoeuvres. For 11 or 12 years I never missed a single game home or away. I've travelled from Rochdale to Rio watching my football, my team, pre-season friendlies, testimonials, European tours, World Cups etc. and our spare room looks like a mini museum. The last thing I or any decent United fan would want is to do anything to offend the club.

But the people who run football have offended the fans often enough in the past.

The 11th February '92 seemed a normal sort of day, when a friend showed me an article about United on the sports pages of a national tabloid. Can you imagine the shock I had when I saw my name mentioned in the opening paragraph? A large section of my letter was being used in a double page spread – most people just get a mention on the sports £10 best letter page.

At the time the Stretford End was about to be demolished at the end of the season and the club announced admission price increases, more than half way through what turned out to be a very difficult season. It outraged thousands of fans. A few weeks earlier the paper had done a piece about bond schemes and price increases at various clubs and they said it was always the fans who suffered at the end of the day.

I wrote to various people at the club, unfortunately this time with no reply except from one director Mr Nigel Burrows (and we all know he had problems of his own). So what other choices do the fans have if the club choose to ignore their supporters' pleas and emotions are running high? Like thousands of others I wrote to the Manchester Evening News and phoned Piccadilly Radio phone-ins. Anyone who may have been able to get some answers to our questions, even the Prime Minister, himself a football fan, took time to give me a straightforward reply – not the one I had liked, but a reply nevertheless.

Anyway, I wasn't notified of the article in the paper. From that morning on, all day my wife was taking calls and messages and when I got home it never stopped, one after another: "Did you see? Have you read?" At first it was exciting. I thought: "Gordon Bennett!" It was like a snowball gaining speed overtaking events and getting too big to handle, but the fans needed all the backing they could get. David Meek, Granada Reports and Tom Tyrell were all reporting on events – the fans were upset. A group called Hostage had organised a meeting for the fans to attend at Lancashire Cricket Club. Manchester United are big news, so a David v Goliath story was food and drink to the media.

There was nothing derogatory in the article that hadn't been previously documented for all to see many times before. It was common knowledge to the fans. I don't believe I brought the honour of the club into disrepute. Numerous people have written and said far more damaging and derogatory things than I. If you want to see the article you'll have to go and dig it up in the Central Library.

Sorry, no Room

I'm trying to tell you the basics here, about the club I love, but we thought thousands of us were

1O DOWNING STREET
LONDON SW1A 2AA

27 February 1992

From the Correspondence Secretary

Dear Mr Donoghue,

The Prime Minister has asked me to thank you for your letter dated 21 February together with the enclosures. This is receiving attention and a reply will be sent to you as soon as possible.

Yours sincerely,

being evicted from our spiritual home – the Stretford End. We were thinking they'd left us to fight among ourselves, for the few remaining spaces in a reduced capacity stadium. Will I get in? Won't I? What about the guys who I've stood next to all my growing years since school? Will they get in as well or be split up to the four corners of the stadium or worse still, split up never ever able to get back in at all?

The Stretford End was special to us – the very heart of the theatre of dreams to generations of fans and the club – our club were saying: "Sorry, no room". There are many ways they could have accommodated those loyal fans. They could have left the United Road a standing area and campaigned harder to keep the Stretford End a standing terrace, but what's done is done.

We all know the fans haven't always seen eye to eye with our chairman and directors as at most clubs, but the majority, contrary to the board's beliefs,

were more concerned about seeing their team than the price increases. Even though they branded the fans "Rebels" and went on about the "price is right", don't they get it? The fans would sell their grannies to get a ticket to see United. We've always found the money from somewhere, sacrificing anything and everything to get in to see our boys.

It is said if United were to play on the moon, the fans would be there waiting for them. But when you can't even get in to

DEPARTMENT OF NATIONAL HERITAGE
Horse Guards Road, London SW1P 3AL

NEWS RELEASE

NOT FOR PUBLICATION, BROADCAST, OR USE ON CLUB TAPES BEFORE 15.30 hrs on 4|6|92. THIS DOCUMENT IS ISSUED IN ADVANCE ON THE STRICT UNDERSTANDING THAT NO APPROACH BE MADE TO ANY ORGANISATION OR PERSON ABOUT ITS CONTENTS BEFORE THE TIME OF PUBLICATION

DNH 13/92
4 June 1992

ALL-SEATING REQUIREMENTS AT FOOTBALL LEAGUE GROUNDS
TO BE RECONSIDERED

David Mellor, Secretary of State for National Heritage, today announced that he is to reconsider the all-seating requirements at Third and Fourth Division clubs in the Football League.

The position of Second Division clubs with very low average attendances will also be re-examined.

But Mr Mellor told the House of Commons that no changes are proposed to the principle and timetable for introducing all-seating at First Division grounds (the new Premier League) and the majority of Second Division clubs. "It must be a priority that our top clubs meet the standards necessary to compete in Europe and provide grounds of which we can all be proud" he said.

And he added that the safety of members of the public attending football matches remained paramount.

1

your home games because every other few years the capacity is reduced even further, you start to ask: Why?

Some fans were concerned about the price increases and rightly so. As a lifelong fan, I always found the money from somewhere to see my team but now I have to pick and choose the away matches I intend to go and see. If the costs of watching football keep rising, I'm wondering just how long it will be before fans start to pick and choose the home games they'll go and see, also. It's already started for cup games, friendlies and testimonials.But the majority at the time were just worried about not getting in.

The Other Old Trafford

Along came the meeting at the cricket club on a cold, wet, dark winter's evening. The other Old Trafford's car park was filling up as if Kerry Packer's pyjama boys were about to googlie a few under the floodlights of the famous Lancashire ground. Inside, the place was packed to the rafters with well over 1,000 fans and, to our amazement, the meeting was chaired by that lovable character, James H. Reaves from Piccadilly Radio.

He wasn't there to give the station's views but to ensure everyone got a fair crack of the whip at the microphone. Also the organisers wanted someone who was not a United fan but understood how the fans felt about the situation, and you can't get further from a die hard Red than the unbiased radio presenter himself.

He told a few jokes like: "I'm sure the day will come when 10,000 fans are locked out at Maine Road" which brought raucous laughter from the audience. We won't go into the rest of them otherwise – how did he put it? – "Now I'll be as unpopular with City fans as I am with United fans". Seriously though, he did a good job getting everybody in a lighthearted frame of mind.

It wasn't anything at all like the club expected – a lynch mob waiting to tear any club representative limb from limb. It was orderly and respectful except for one or two who were obviously very angry, but that was understandable under the circumstances. Anyway, the organisers and the fans conducted themselves with decorum and in the true spirit that Manchester United fans are rarely credited for.

A lot of people spoke from the heart about our club with genuine passion and I was fortunate to be one of them who got to speak at the microphone. I said something on the lines of: "We don't want a theatre of broken dreams, we want the board to stand up and say: 'Our club stamp is Manchester United the world's greatest football club. So let's prove it, let's give our loyal fans a stadium they can be proud of and not locked out of'".

When the applause died down I added that they have a quote of the week in the programme and I'd give them one if they'd print it: Football is a great game, the only game that unites the world and its supporters and it's they who make it a great game. Football without them is nothing and the sooner the people who run the game realise that, the better it will be for each and everyone of us". And that was made by Jock Stein in 1967.

That quote was well received within the Lancashire Lounge. Various other Reds spoke at length, people from fanzines and obviously the organisers from the Hostage group, now USA (United Supporters Association). But I can't comment on them because I don't have a transcript of the evening – just my diary notes, as we fans saw it at the time.

Later I said cheerio to a few friends and at the end of the evening after all the emotional speeches, late into the wet and blustery night, I got in my car, called at the United Chippy on Chester Road then parked up on the club's forecourt under the fluorescent sign that glowed red and shimmering on the wet concrete below. It was going on towards midnight and here was I all alone, day dreaming of the hundreds of times I'd walked down the Warwick Road and into virtually every part of that grand old stadium, laughed, cried and cheered 'till I was hoarse. I couldn't believe my club, yes my club was going to turn thousands of us away.

That quote I made earlier from Jock Stein was the one that I sent to Mr Edwards in gold ink on a black background, framed, as a small gift for him to keep on his desk as a reminder. I don't know if the chairman has kept it in his office or it has taken a slam dunk into the waste paper basket, but he was kind enough to reply to my letter. Despite the hard time we were having at the time with Ron Atkinson as manager, he thanked me for the gift and loyal support through both the good and bad times.

I don't see myself as a Victor Meldrew or Rab C. Nesbitt character. But like most British people I think we are a fair nation and when something is seen to be unfair, then it's our God-given right to question and, if need be, protest until a settlement or agreement has been found. I and many others have been campaigning since early 1973 to try and appeal to the club to either cantilever or double tier the Stretford End, as we could see the stands creeping round to us over the years. It was inevitable that our beloved terrace would eventually cop it (oops! don't say that) – but in what shape and form? Up and over like Real Madrid's Bernabeu, or up and up like Twickenham?

If we can build a tunnel with executive suites above, we can build one over the United Road like Barcelona's Nou Camp on one side. I can hear the board screaming: "Who's going to finance this dream?" When you think of certain office blocks in the City costing £25M to £40M and then you think how much our club means to the people of Manchester and beyond, with a name known around the world, there isn't a banker in the whole of Europe wouldn't back any plans the club had.

Surely between Mr Edwards, Mr Midani and the rest of the board they could persuade numerous backers (oops! don't say that either) I mean bankers in the City to put up the funds needed. I mean, the fans will never turn their backs on the club and if United keep turning over profits like they do year after year, any loan could be paid back in less than half of your average mortgage by the successors of the board.

As I said, as the years went by we could see the stadium taking shape. The Stretford End sweeping back majestically with a panoramic view and a members' lounge behind would have made Old Trafford better than Wembley – it is anyway in my view. Of course, none of us had a crystal ball and could see the Taylor Report coming, but our worries were eased when I received another letter from the chairman assuring the fans that the wishes of the supporters in that area would be taken into very careful consideration before any developments were decided. That also was read out at the cricket club meeting I spoke of earlier.

There's a lot to be said for referendums on important issues that affect the supporters, especially when the issue splits the board's vote enough that someone has to play God with people's lives. Bill Shankly I think said: "Football isn't a matter of life or death, it's much more important than that". If the club don't expand or move they'll lose a whole generation of supporters forever. They'll go and watch another local club or rugby, go ten pin bowling or play Gameboys on a Saturday afternoon and they will learn to miss the games without regret.

I believe Martin Edwards is a man doing his best in a very difficult job, but if he does have a PR man, there's room for improvement, because at times our chairman has been made as welcome as a new egg in the Jurassic Park laboratories. Nobody's asking him to kowtow to pressure or to consult the fans before every transaction, that's ludicrous. But our support has never wavered once in this 26-year wait. We are constantly told this is "our club, a family club" and "no one man is bigger than the club". Don't we deserve a bit of consideration on such important issues?

This club, like no other in this country, is as close to the fans' hearts as a member of their own family. It's there in our lives always. Cars, houses, pubs, friends, all come and go, but the club is an anchor. I'm sure if you blindfolded 99% of all Reds they'd find their way to OT before home, work, the pub, anywhere. If suddenly that which they hold most dear was taken away from them, what would you expect them to do?

The club have the perfect platform in the United Review to reply to any adverse criticism the fans may direct at them. We deserve straight answers to honest heartfelt questions, and if the club avoid answering those questions, the fans will tug away at their heels like a fox terrier until they get some answers. The Prime Minister and the England Manager have to answer to the people and the media, so why should the people who run our club be any different?

The chairman was on the radio reminding us that if the board had listened to the fans' views we would be looking at a new manager yet again. But he neglected to point out that we may not have had a club at all if the board had listened to a certain 'late' newspaper magnate. That's one of the reasons why the fanzines sprung up so quickly. They're not just a satirical, humorous way of looking at the clubs we all love. They were and still are willing to listen to and put forward the fans' views.

There are only so many schemes and ideas they can come up with before the bubble bursts. And as for all the rule changes like the back pass and foreign players, and suggestions like taking kick-ins instead of throw-ins. Well! The game is pure and simple and it's a beautiful game when it's played right. There's no other sport in the world that can touch it, never mind equal it. How many fans, players and managers, have their little superstitions that they do week in week out and

God help anyone that interferes with it? The message is clear: if you've got a winning combination don't mess with it.

I don't wish to seem like I'm on a soap box on Hyde Park Corner, but if the powers that be want to try and understand the way the fans feel, they'd do well to read this chapter if nothing else. I don't profess to be anyone special. Like thousands of others, I'm just an ordinary bloke who follows his team, through thick and thin, and I thought I'd write a book. I've never done it before. I got 30-odd other Reds to help me put together various different views on the same subject, and like a Mori Poll we've come up with a consensus of opinion about a club and the game we all dearly love to see.

And if, by any chance, we upset the club or chairmen, it's only because they sometimes make such outrageous decisions. The fans have no other choice but to demonstrate their feelings in the only way they know how – by writing to the club, ringing radio phone-ins or the TV and press media. Believe me, the clubs have all the power. At the touch of a button on a mobile phone they can summon the whole media circus, so don't tell me they can't take our views and feelings into consideration as though we weren't accessible.

So Mr Edwards, Mr Parry, Mr Sky and Mr Umbro, couldn't you just for once listen and act upon your customers' requests? Maybe, just maybe, the harmony between clubs and supporters could be restored and your foot will be comfortably pampered in perfectly tailored boots...football boots of course!

Now that my beloved Stretford End has gone, like most fans I refuse to call it the new West Stand. The fans are not over the moon that the best central block has been handed over to the executive lounge set at a price very few of last season's Stretford Enders would ever be able to afford. Do I see that finger near the self destruct button again? I do hope the set don't start to spread out and take old Stretford End fans' places.

Fergie said the spiritual heart of the stadium will never be the same again and it will take some getting used to, but would I sacrifice the cherished memories of the theatre of dreams for a dream theatre? I'm not sure, because I could be selfish and say stuff it, I've got my plastic pop-up seat. But what about all those who have been going for years but can no longer get in? And that includes the away fans – they are part of the atmosphere as well. At the moment, the club is

Uniterd R Back, says the banner, but isn't it time we had a second National stadium in the north – preferably Manchester?

THANK YOU!

United's fans put the smile back in soccer

By Peter Spencer

THE magnificent, triumphant Manchester United Red Army were today showered with praise.

As their team scored a glorious 2-1 Euro victory against Barcelona last night, the fans were notching up their own brand of glory for soccer and their home city.

Today the thanks came pouring in — from both sides of the Channel.

THANK YOU. The Prime Minister sent a message to United manager Alex Ferguson. Mr Major said: "Your team's performance and your supporters' behaviour showed the best elements of the English game to Europe.

"I very much hope that next season the number of European trophies coming to the United Kingdom will increase."

THANK YOU. Rotterdam chief constable Rob Hessing said: "It's been a pleasure welcoming the United supporters to our city — they can come back every week!"

The Rotterdam police even faxed the *Evening News*, saying: "Supporters of Manchester United — thank you for your understanding co-operation, co-operation and your sporting attitude."

Reds are Simply the best

UNITED stars were enjoying long lie-ins in their "fortress" luxury hotel, five miles from the centre of Rotterdam.

A celebration party, attended by fanatical Reds supporter Mick Hucknall, lead singer with Simply Red, went on until the early hours.

The flame-haired singer, who has a home a stone's throw from Old Trafford, did not perform at the celebratory bash, held in the Elysee Park Hotel, which was guarded by private security guards.

Rock star Phil Collins was reported by the Dutch press to be the VIP guest at the United camp's party, but he did not show up.

Hucknall, 30, who was later today leaving Holland for Los Angeles, where he is booked into a studio to record his new album, was said to be "over the moon."

THANK YOU. Rotterdam Mayor Bram Peper, who had thought of cancelling the European Cup Winners' final because of crowd trouble fears, said: "The fans behaviour was exceptionally good.

THANK YOU: Reds' manager Ferguson said: "I knew our people would not let us down. I knew they wouldn't spoil the party."

THANK YOU: Skipper Bryan Robson said: "The fans were impeccable."

Sir Matt Busby, president of United, joined in the praise, saying: "It was like the old days."

Reds' chairman Martin Edwards said: "The supporters' behaviour was always going to be as important as the actual match and we seem to have come out winners on both counts."

Match star Steve Bruce said: "Our crowd were unbelievable. It was a wet night but they outshouted the opposition." Sports minister Robert Atkins predicted "a new era" for English fans.

The supporters "were a credit to the country and to themselves."

The fans' superb behaviour helped to ease the pain of other European soccer memories. They removed any doubts Europe had about the readmission of English clubs.

Only five of the 25 supporters arrested were English.

Greater Manchester assistant chief constable Malcolm George said in Rotterdam: "United fans have caused no problems. The Dutch police are delighted."

Fans returning to Manchester airport from Rotterdam also won praise from police.

Picture special: Pages 2,3
Comment: Page 6

From the *Manchester Evening News,* May 16 1991: reproduced with permission

getting tit-for-tat tactics for away match ticket allocations, so we fans have very little choice but to miss some games or sit at OT and watch closed circuit TV which isn't the same as being there.

Even Alex Ferguson said recently on TV that he's forever getting on to his chairman about building on what we've got. It won't be easy but if his calculations are right we could do it. This club needs a 60,000 seater stadium. We shouldn't forget who we are – our roots – and we can't have this ridiculous situation where many, many supporters are going to be locked out or paying touts five, six or ten times more than the face value of a ticket because of their desire to get in to see their team. It's outrageous!

Nearly 96,000 members can't fit into a 45,000 seater stadium which looks good as an architect's dream, but to be blunt, it's just not big enough. More often than not, United could fill a 60,000 to 70,000 seater stadium easy, especially for Derbys, big games and European matches. For every one fan at the game there are at least another 10 in the pub watching it on TV who say: "What's the point in going down, we've no chance of getting in".

Last season thousands of fans were locked out, and now even more people will want to see the champions. Remember, these views are only what the fans are saying, in the bars and clubs around the city and probably the UK – suggestions that have been put to me while researching for this book. I'm sure a large percentage of all United supporters would love to stay at Old Trafford and build on what we've got.

Our stadium is one of the finest in Europe. Most of the so-called all-seater stadia abroad have no roof, no refreshment area and, to be honest, no seats. They just have concrete steps with a bit of lattice wood bolted down and a painted number – the supporters then just stand up on it anyway. Our fans have been all over Europe and very rarely do you see a stadium as good as Old Trafford. Even the larger grounds have their drawbacks: either you are in a corner with a restricted view or you are so high up that apart from the colour of the kits you can't tell which ant is which player. It could be Curly, Larry and Mo playing out there for all we know (yes I know at times, we feel like it is).

Our theatre of dreams is special to us and all we are asking is to make Old Trafford large enough again to accommodate its own loyal supporters who have stuck by the club through the years. I mean if they want to raise more revenue there's nothing to stop them renting out space under the stands to companies like Mac-Donalds or Kentucky Fried Chicken. They could have mini bars named after famous players sponsored by Boddingtons or Bells with Sharp video or TV screens relaying the game so you don't miss anything if you have to nip for a pie or a pee. If it's good enough for Real Madrid's Bernabeu it's good enough for United's OT, and anyway why should those privileges be for the executive suites only? Surely Sharp, the club's sponsors could spare a few TV screens.

When we went to Rotterdam we saw a closed circuit diamond video screen on a mobile trailer similar to the one United had on the pitch for the City and Palace games. It showed the game to all the Reds who couldn't get into the Feyenoord stadium. Someone on the board of directors could note this and request that our sponsors – one of the biggest electronic firms in the world – might park one on Sir Matt Busby Way for big games. Then, if, er... when thousands are locked out as last season – especially at the Blackburn game, they won't be so disappointed after travelling miles to try and get in.

The French club Marseille did it outside for the European Cup Final and so did the Dutch for us. So come on United, play the game. If our stadium can't accommodate all our members, at least show them you are willing to help them see their team. The video screen could pay for itself by advertising Sharp products or Coca Cola or something.

Clubs could also save money if they weren't held to ransom by certain clubs and player's agents who demand ridiculous transfer fees. There used to be a ceiling (unofficial) a few years ago where transfer fees were levelling out, but once Spurs sold Gascoigne and Lineker, the fees just went through the roof again. Nobody is worth 6, 15 or even 30 million, not even our own Ryan Giggs. Looking at some of the players today you might ask: "Well if that Italian or Brazilian is worth that much what would Georgie Best in his prime be worth today?"

Not even Manchester United have a bottomless pit of money and if things carry on the way they are, pretty soon they'll price out the normal working class spectator and then they will have killed the goose that laid the golden egg. But it will be too late then, and as before, we will then say: "We told you so" ...but would you listen? Only time will tell.

Home-coming Parades

The final paragraphs in this chapter are taken up by a subject that has also come about these last five or six years, and will be a real bee in the bonnet to all United and probably City supporters, next time they win anything. I'm referring to the traditional home coming parade with the trophies to Albert Square and the town hall. Every other club in the country take their spoils back to the fans and parade them in all their glory, with speeches and waves to the fans, family and friends. What has our club or the council done to spoil this tradition that goes back to the days of the horse drawn carriages when Manchester United greeted their fans in the square?

The lame excuse was: "We've just had the square reflagged, paved and landscaped and it needs time to flourish". That was six years ago and in that time they've had everything in there: the Milk Race, Chinese New Year parades, gay marches, animal rights campaigners, Lord Mayor's parades, Maxwell pensioners' protests and the ones that make the most mess – Christmas and New Year's Eve revellers in their thousands.

We're not saying that's wrong but you know the council with their "job's worth" award

Patiently they waited in the pouring rain in Deansgate, Manchester

Then along came the conquering heroes.

And we, as always, followed – singing in the rain

employees: "It's more than my job's worth to give you that information" etc. For God's sake, we also elect these people and pay their wages to serve us, the public (does that sound familiar?). They can't or won't give the reason why United and City aren't allowed in the square with their trophies and fans. Rubbish! we say.

If I were the club I'd put my foot down and say no to the civic receptions. Why should the Lord Mayor and all the knobs get to see the trophies and mingle with the players close up? Yet fans have to scramble for the best vantage point on a pub or office window ledge along Deansgate in the pouring rain, not hearing the manager and players' speeches and congratulations.

It used to be a great occasion especially for all the fans who couldn't get tickets for whatever final. Now it's a whizz past on an open top bus and we've waited patiently and orderly for hours for a few seconds fleeting glimpse. At least in Albert Square we got to see the damn trophy and players for 20 minutes or so after our long wait. And the TV people would do a half hour special of the home coming. Now what do we get? A 60-second clip shoved in between Elton Welsby and Fred the weatherman!

Surely United could come to some agreement with the council or bring our trophies back to Salford or Trafford. I'm sure those councils would appreciate and find room for the club that brings pride, glory and prestige to the city. And I'm sure "Mr Jobsworth" wouldn't like that.

10

MUSIC TO MY EARS

We Red Devils may not be the Vienna Boys Choir or the Welsh Valleys' finest but for most Reds, to hear the massed ranks of United's Red Army in full cry is better than Pavarotti, Sinatra, U2 and Queen put together.

The history of football songs and their origins is vague to say the least. Groups of people have sung songs in small and large gatherings for various reasons and occasions since time immemorial. It's widely accepted that footy songs originated in the pubs and clubs during and just after the Second World War to keep up morale in what was obviously a very emotional and difficult period in our country's history. There's not a person on this planet who hasn't been touched by the words or the tune of a song at some time in their lives.

The very nature of the football song is not unlike that of the crude joke or the rugby song – acceptable in its right place and at the right time. If we are all honest, most of us swear at some time or other – even Princess Anne has her bad days. But football has its own brand of humour and be it right or wrong it has a reputation as a hard game. It's a man's game, one in which there is no quarter asked or given.

Men and women can go on what used to be a traditional Saturday afternoon (are you listening Sky?) and let off some steam, sing a few songs, have a laugh and a chat and enjoy one another's company knowing there's something that unites them all for a few hours each week. It is escapism from the mundane chores most of us have to endure – work – and oh yes, if we're lucky we might even get to see a good game of footy to boot!

Have you noticed football songs are universal wherever the beautiful game is played? It's amazing how you can travel around the world and hear the same songs and chants sung by a million other supporters in a thousand different languages with the same fervour.

Forget technology – support live music!

And it's not just with the development of satellite, TV or radio that these songs are spread. How do you explain that a song or chant can be thought up and sung at say Torquay United or Crewe and soon it's repeated up and down the country by other clubs' supporters re-mixed to suit their particular team? Did you notice as soon as Marseille won the European Cup that their fans were singing Queen's "We are the champions"? Now I wonder where they heard that? At Holland's World Cup qualifying game against Norway, their fans were all into "Always look on the bright side of life" – nothing to do with half of Holland watching us in Rotterdam I suppose?

Here we have some United songs and chants or at least our version of them by the unknown supporter, one or two of which my mates and I actually claim to have made up in various public houses, train specials or airport departure lounges over the years. In our inebriated state we may have even picked up a line here or a tune there subconsciously and then claimed it as our own, but that's half the fun of it.

Some are rubbish and some are sheer bliss – "music to my ears". If you don't know them already, learn them and teach them to your children. Better still get your friends to buy this book and let them learn the songs themselves. The next time you come to the Mecca of football, Old Trafford, or you are following the Reds away or on foreign soil, sing your hearts out for the lads. Oh! and don't forget the Tunes for the throat.

For obvious reasons we haven't included some of the more vulgar and lurid songs and chants because this is basically a humorous sports related book and not one for the top shelf.

Walkin' down the Warwick Road

Oh me lads, you should have seen us cummin'
Fastest team in the league just to see us runnin'
All me lads and lasses smiles upon their faces
Walkin' down the Warwick Road
To see Matt Busby's Aces
Repeat till fade

> (Home and away, late 50s and early 60s to present day. Adaptation of *The Bladen Races*)

We shall not be moved (chant)

We shall not, we shall not be moved
We shall not, we shall not be moved
Just like a team that's gonna win
The Football League (again) or FA Cup (again)
We shall not be moved.

> (Home and away '67 and by the early 90s. 24th year we were paranoid at singing it but it will be back with a vengeance now.)

Cryin' Over You

Cryin' over you
Cryin' over you,
Now that its gone (the title)
And you're standin all alone,
Alone and cryin', cryin', cryin'
Cryin',
Cryin' over you, (fade out)

> (Half time home game v Leeds, 2-0 up very early in '93 season. Adaptation of Roy Orbison song)

"Onward Red Soldiers" (chant)

Onward Man United Boot Boys
marching as to war
with the flag of United going on before.

"Stretford Enders"

Bertie Mee said to Don Revie
have you heard of the North Bank Highbury,
No said Don I don't think so,
but I've heard of the Stretford Enders,
Na na nan nan na nan nan nan na.

> (Home and away, especially at Highbury mid-60s)

"The Bells"

The bells are ringing for Docherty's boys,
the bells are ringing for Docherty's boys,
Man United are scoring,
The Stretford End roaring,
Stuart Pearson puts four in,
we'll be happy again.
The bells are ringing for Docherty's boys.
Repeat till fade

> (2nd div. ditty sung to 'For Me and My Girl')

The King

We'll drink a drink a drink,
To Denis the King, the King, the King
For he's the leader of our football team
He's the greatest centre forward
That the world has ever seen

We'll drink a drink, a drink,
To Denis the King, the King, the King
For he is, our super ace
For he invented the vertical take off,
Now he's learning how to fly.
We'll drink a drink, a drink
To Denis the King, the King, the King,
Repeat till fade

> (Tune: *Lily the Pink* – Scaffold '69)

"Viva Bobby Charlton" (chant)

Bobby Charlton viva Bobby Charlton,
Bobby Charlton viva Bobby Charlton,
viva, viva!
Bobby Charlton and his soccer team oh yeah!
Everybody's gonna see a sensation,
a sensation, a sensation, hear what I say now,
Bobby Charlton viva Bobby Charlton,
Fade. . . .

> *Viva Bobby Joe* tune - The Equals '69 hit)

"Stick Together"

For United we stand City they fall,
come on you devils lets stay on the ball,
let's stick together.
come on, come on, lets stick together, now, now, people,
because together we can stand,
every boy, girl, woman and man.
ooh all together, ooh all together, ooh all together.

> (Mid-70s adaptation of *Let's Stick Together* – Bryan Ferry)

I was Born under the Stretford End

I was born under the Stretford End,
I was born under the Stretford End,
Where boots were made for kickin',
And braces are made to pull
Levis are made for bleachin' and the jackets are as well.
I was born under the Stretford End,
I was born under the Stretford End
Do I know where hell is, hell is in Maine Road
Heaven is whenever Uni-ted score a goal.
I was born under the Stretford End,
. . . Repeat till fade

(Adaptation of 1970 tune, *Wanderin' Star* –
Lee Marvin)

I'd Walk a Million Miles "Denis Law/Stuart Pearson" (chant)

Oh Oh Oh Denis, Denis ,(waving both hands)
I'd walk a million miles for one of your goals
Oh Denis
Oh Oh Oh Stuart, Stuart, (waving both hands)
I'd walk a million miles for one of your goals
Oh Stuart

(Adaptation of Al Jolson's *Mammy*. Home
and away 60s and 70s)

Just One of Those Teams

We are just one of those teams
That you will see now and then,
We often score six but we like to score ten,
We beat 'em at home and we beat 'em away,
We'll beat anybody that get in our way.
We are the pride of all Europe
The cock of the North
We beat the Scousers and Cockneys of course.
We are United without any doubt,
We are the Manchester boys
La la la la la la la la
La la la la la la oooh!

(Present day adaptation of Ethel Merman
song. A classic Hollywood tune)

Que Sera Sera

When I was just a little boy,
I asked my daddy what will I be,
Will I be blue will I be red
Here's what he said to me.
You're a red my boy,
And you are my pride and joy,
The reds are the team we'll see,
Que sera sera.
Que sera sera we are the reds you see,
We're going to Wembley,
Que sera sera
Que sera sera, whatever will be, will be
We're going to Wembley, Que Sera Sera.

(A Doris Day tune, *Que sera sera*.
Leicester City away 75/76 in the FA Cup.
Pity we only sing the last verse these days)

Ryan Giggs (chant)

Ryan Giggs, Ryan Giggs, running down the wing,
Ryan Giggs, Ryan Giggs, running down the wing,
Feared by the blues, loved by the reds,
Ryan Giggs clap clap clap,
Ryan Giggs clap clap clap,
Ryan Giggs clap clap clap.
(Repeat till fade)

(Sung to the *Robin Hood* tune)

Over and Over

Over and Over we will follow you,
Over and over we will see you through,
We're United Supporters faithful through and through,
Over and over, we will follow you.
If you go to Germany we'll go once again,
France or Spain it's all the same,
We'll go anywhere.
If you need supportin', you will always know,
We'll be right there with you, everywhere you go.
Over and over, we will follow you.
Over and over, we will see you through,
We're United supporters faithful through and through,
Over and over we will follow you.

(Adapted from the Celtic song *Over and
Over*. In pub before and after Bryan
Robson's testimonial and at Anfield away
end of season '92)

Wembley May Day 68

We went down to Wembley one fine day in May
Where all our supporters were merry and gay
And when it was over and when it was done
We defeated Benfica by 4 goals to 1.
The first came from Bobby, he out jumped the rest,
The second came from wee Georgie Best,
The fans went quite crazy, they roared United
The third came from 19 year old, the young Brian
  Kidd.
The crowd were all chanting and shouting for more,
So Bobby obliged by making it four.
A night I'll remember and always recall,
Man United the greatest of all.

> (Obviously a favourite heard in Albert
> Square just a few days after the '68 final)

Wembley May Day 77

We went down to Wembley one fine day in May,
Where all our supporters were merry and gay
And when it was over, and when it was done,
We defeated Liverpool by 2 goals to 1.
The first one went in by our big Stu,
The second went in by you know who
And Greenhoff is magic and Greenhoff is ace,
And he put the Scousers right in their place.

> (Liverpool away '78 after United stopped
> Liverpool winning the treble)

Ooh Arh Cantona (chant)

Ooh arrh, Ooh arrh, Ooh arrh Can-to-na
Ooh arrh la Cantona
  (Tune of the Marseillaise)
Ooh arrh, Cantona, we've got your Cantona,
Ooh arrh, Cantona, we've got your Cantona.

> (Tune of *Oops Upside Your Head*. 1980 hit of
> The Gap Band)

Oh Come all ye Faithful

Oh come all ye faithful,
Come ye oh come ye to Old Trafford.
Come and behold him (Denis Law)
Born the king of football.
Oh come let us adore him,
Oh come let us adore him,
Oh come let us adore him,
Denis the King.

> (1965 onwards after Denis scored and was
> crowned king of the Stretford End)

Last Bus from Amsterdam

When it's spring again, we'll sing again,
Last bus from Amsterdam,
When we're soaking through and sinking too
Last bus from Amsterdam.
As long as our boys, keep on scoring
The whole bus keeps on roaring,
So till we see the Red lights again,
We'll be the last bus from Amsterdam.

> (Tune – Max Bygraves' *Tulips from Amster-*
> *dam*. Ajax away '76, as our bus nearly
> reversed out of the open ferry doors we
> made this up. It was sung all through the
> match and on the ferry crossing home)

Wild Red Rover

I've been a red devil for many a year
And I've spent all my money on whiskey and beer
Singing Man-U-nited, Man United F.C.
We're by far the greatest team
The world has ever seen.
And it's Man-U-nited, Man United F.C.
Repeat till fade

> (Waterford away Euro Cup 1st round '69,
> brought home to OT on ferry by Irish Reds)

The Red Flag

Division one can kiss my arse,
We're in Division two at last,
We don't mind and we don't care
We'll keep the red flag flyin' there.
The City fans came out of school,
Manchester was theirs to rule,
But they found to their despair
That the red flag was still there.
The football league should listen well
Of what United have to tell,
Macari, Doc and Sammy Mac,
Division one we're coming back.
So when you're down and feeling blue,
Because we're in division two,
Don't you fret and don't you cry,
We'll keep the red flag flyin' high.
Will never die, will never die,
Will never die, will never die,
We'll keep the red flag flyin' high,
Cos, Man United will never die.

> (Home and away late 50s after the air crash,
> commemorating the Phoenix rising from the
> ashes and home and away '75 after United's
> relegation. One of the finest songs ever, and
> once again only the last verse remains)

Scarlet Ribbon

She wore, she wore, she wore a scarlet ribbon,
She wore a scarlet ribbon the that fine day in May,
And when I asked her why, she wore that ribbon
She said it's for United 'cos they're going to Wembley.
Wembley, Wembley.
We're the famous Man United and we're going to
  Wembley.

(1977 semi-final v Leeds at Hillsboro. Tune
from American Western film)

Skip to my Lou (chant)

Who put the ball in the West Ham net,
Who put the ball in the West Ham net,
Who put the ball in the West Ham net,
Skip to my Lou Macari,
Lou, Lou skip to my Lou,
Lou, Lou skip to my Lou,
Lou, Lou skip to my lou,
Skip to my Lou Macari.
(After Lou's first goal at West Ham '73)

Six Foot Two (chant)

Six foot, two eyes of blue
Big Him Holton's after you,
Na na nan na na nan na nan na.
Six foot two eyes of blue
Big Jim Holton's after you,
Na na nan na nan na nan na na.

(A folk hero to the Reds. United never lost
when he played in the team '75, or did they?)

Stretford End Picnic

If you come down to the Stretford End
You better not come alone.
If you come down to the Stretford End
You better come in disguise.
For all the fans that ever there was
Are gathered there today because
Today's the day, the day we play Man City.
If you come down to the Stretford End
You're sure for a big surprise.
If you come down to the Stretford End
You would not believe your eyes.
For all the reds that ever there was
Are gathered there today because,
Today's the day, the day we slay Man City.

(Tune *Teddy Bears Picnic*)

The Sunbed Song (chant)

I'm too sexy for my shirt, so sexy it hurts,
I'm too sexy for Milan
Too sexy for Milan, Bermuda and Oldham.

(Not heard at OT but in the bars around
town. Fans will know which player the
chant's about. Adaptation of *Right Said Fred*)

United is our Name

Who won the league with a ten point lead,
  we did, we did.
Who won the league with a ten point lead,
  United is our name.
United is our name, United is our name,
We won the league with a ten point lead
United is our name.

(Tune to the Camptown Races. There's a
similar one about City and the number 17
isn't there boys and girls!)

Those Were the Days

Those were the days my friend,
We thought they'd never end,
We'd sing and dance forever and a day.
We'd live the life we choose,
We'd fight and never lose,
Cos we're the Stret
We are the Stretford End.
We are the Stretford End,
And we are round the bend.
We'll sing and dance forever and a day,
We'll live the life we choose,
We'll fight and never lose,
Cos we're the Stret
We are the Stretford End.

(A long-time favourite since '68 onwards.
An adaptation of the Mary Hopkins song)

The Banks of the River Irwell

From the banks of the River Irwell
To the shores of Sicilly.
We will fight, fight, fight for United,
Till we win the football league.
To hell with Liverpool
To hell with Man City (they're sh..)
We will fight, fight for United,
Till we win the football league.
(Repeat till fade)

(Tune *Halls of Montezuma*...home and away
mid-60s onwards)

Always Look on the Bright Side of Life!

Always look on the bright side of life,
De do, de do, de do, de do,
Always look on the bright side of life,
De do, de do, de do, de do,
City are sh.. when you look at it,
All they do is lose and moan and whinge,
When you're feeling in the dumps,
Don't be silly chumps.
Just look across at City and you'll sing,
Oh! Always look on the bright side of life,
(whistle) de do, de do, de do, de do.
Repeat till fade

> (Montpelier away '91. Eric Idle classic)

Forever and Ever

Forever and ever we'll follow the boys,
Of Man United the Busby Babes.
For we made a promise to follow thee
A part time supporter, I never shall be.
Forever and ever we'll follow thee
And Man United to victory.
Their names are now legend
For the whole world to see.
The club's a religion spelt M.U.F.C.
Forever and ever we'll keep the faith,
Of Man United and the Busby Babes.

> (Home games late 50s and early 60s up to the present day)

Georgie Best (chant)

Georgie Best super star, how many goals
Have you scored so far?
Georgie Best super star, how many girls
Have you had so far?
Alternate chants till fade

> (Tune – *Jesus Christ Superstar* theme. Home and away games after the Miss World incident early 70s)

Hello, Hello

Hello, hello, we are the Busby Boys.
Hello, hello, we are the Busby Boys.
And if you are a City fan
Surrender or you'll die.
We will follow United, hello, hello!
Repeat at least three times

> (Tune – *Marching through Georgia*. Mid-60s home and away to present day)

Hail Hail United

Hail Hail United's here
And you know we'll be there,
And you know we'll be there,
Hail, hail United's here
And you know we'll be there too.
For it's a grand old team to play for
And it's a grand old team to see,
And if you know the history
It's enough to make your heart go
Oh! Oh! Oh! Oh! We don't care what the City fans
   say
What the hell do we care
For we only know that there's gonna be a show
And that Man United will be there,
And that Man-U-nited will be there,
Shout United, United.

> (Adapted from the Celtic song, most away games, mid 70s onwards to present day)

Blue Moon (Red Mix)

Blue Moon you started singin' too soon,
You thought you beat us 3-1
But Chocky spoilt your fun.
Blue Goons we saw you standin' alone,
Without a team in your heart,
Without a cup of your own.
Blue Moon you started singin' too soon,
You thought you beat us 3-1
Now Howard Kendal has gone.

> (Maine Road away '92 during 3-3 draw. Tune is Rogers and Hart 30/40s classic)

Glory, Glory Man United '93 mix

In 77 it was Docherty,
Ferguson will make it 93
And everyone will know just who we are
We'll be singin' Que Sera Sera.
United, Man United we're the boys in red,
And we know we're gonna win the league,
Win the league, win the league.
We're the famous Man United
And we're gonna win the league.
Glory, Glory Man United,
Glory, Glory Man United.
As the reds go marching
On, On, On -
Repeat till fade

> (Tune of the club's 1983 hit single, in the pubs and clubs in and around OT after Crystal Palace game, on video screen)

United We Stand (chant)

For United we stand
City they fall.
We are the greatest football team of them all.
We'll be together, forever one and all -

(Another half-time favourite when the D.J. played it at O.T. 1970. Brotherhood of Man)

Who's That Team They Call United?

Who's that team they call United?
Who's that team we all adore?
They're the boys in red and white
And we'll fight with all our might,
'cos they want to know the reason why we roar.
Bring on Sunderland and Arsenal,
Bring on Spaniards by the score,
Barcelona, Real Madrid,
They will make a gallant bid.
But we're out to show the world that we can score.
Who's that tappin' on the window?
Who's that knocking on the door?
It's Joe Mercer and his mates,
They've got turkey on their plates,
'cos they can't get into Europe any more.
United clap clap clap United clap clap clap!

(A well-loved song heard not long after Georgie Best's goals in Lisbon '67. Tune American hymn *God Loves All The Little Children*)

Molly Malone

In Salford's fair city,
Where the girls are so pretty,
I first set my eyes on sweet
Molly Malone.
As she wheeled her wheelbarrow
Through the streets broad and narrow, singing
M.U., M.U.F., M.U.F.C., OK.

(Mid 60s home and away. Irish classic)

The Viking (chant)

Schmeichel, Schmeichel,
Or United, United,
The best in all the land and all the world
Repeat two or three times till fade

(Adaptation of the Viking tune from a Kirk Douglas film, first done in 1972 and now rejuvenated after big Peter was voted the world's No. 1 goalie)

There are a few more songs that any United fan worth his salt will never forget. They were sung at two European Finals and celebrations for winning the Championship but are not sung in general at the games.

After the taunts from one or two clubs' envious fans last season, when they chanted "We've never seen United win the league" I've put pen to paper and turned that tune to our advantage and come up with the following. It takes 60 seconds to sing all the way through and is befitting the stature of our boys' achievement.

Let's get some legendary songs going, as we did for Sir Matt and the boys of '67/'68 and the Doc with his swash-bucklers of the '70s. I gave it an airing on our summer hols in Spain and it went down well with Reds we met out there wearing their colours with pride. Let's hope it catches on or someone comes up with something better.

Did you see Man United?

Have you ever seen United win the League?
(shout) Yes we have
Have you ever seen United win the League?
(shout) Yes we have,
Have you ever seen United, ever seen United
Ever seen United win the League?
(shout) Yes we have,
Did you see Bruce's headers?
(shout) Yes we did, Yes we did,
Did you see Fergie jump?
(shout) Yes we did, Yes we did
Did you see Kiddo pray, see Kiddo pray, see Kiddo
pray?
(shout) Yes we did, Yes we did
Did you see Giggsy's goal?
(shout) Yes we did, Yes we did,
Did you see Incy dance?
(shout) Yes we did, Yes we did,

Did you see Pally smile, see Pally smile, see Pally smile
for a mile?
(shout) Yes we did.
Now did you see Man United win the League?
(shout) Yes we did,
Did you see Man United win the League?
(shout) Yes we did,
Did you see Man United, see Man United, see Man
United win the League?
(shout) Yes we did.

(Total time 60 seconds, written by Steve Donoghue on 11th June 1993. To the tune of *She'll be Coming Round the Mountain*)

There's one song we haven't mentioned that is sung from A.C. Milan to Chorley F.C., from Rio to Rochdale. Yes calm down, calm down it's . . . *You'll Never Walk Alone*. This used to be sung by United's army at home and away and the world over. I'm mentioning this only because I used to enjoy seeing our Red's fans out singing and out classing the opposition with our display of colour and character. Remember the display at Robbo's testimonial, and also the spectacular display during the championship game versus Blackburn? Wouldn't that be great every week?

But for some reason it became fashionable not to mention "that song" and "that title" for the simple reason we were getting paranoid towards them both. Well now the hoodoo is gone and the spell, the curse has been broken, don't you think it's about time we gave this one another airing? Blimey, my ears have just spontaneously ignited – does that mean a lot of you out there disagree?

Oh well, a lot of us older fans used to enjoy singing "that song" at Anfield, especially when we'd won there and as I said at the beginning of this chapter, who's to say a song is exclusive to one particular club. "That song" comes from the musical Carousel and was sung by Fulham and Chelsea supporters long before Gerry and the Pacemakers covered it, and the Liverpool fans adopted it as their anthem way back in the '60s.

There are many many more songs and chants that are not here. Apologies to everyone if your particular favourite is not among them, but we've covered a fair few. Remember we all do it, but let's not forget most of it is done in jest and the high spirits of the occasion. All decent fans are trying to bring back the atmosphere and good crack at the games and I know a lot of Reds are purposely avoiding the chants of incitement to our rivals in the hope that the decent element among their followers will do the same when their lot start up.

We all know what I'm getting at, but I'm sure none of us wants to see players' careers cut short through injury or see fans or players dying in the name of football ever again. But no doubt, disasters will always happen, it's human nature and you'll always get a few hot heads trying to wind United up. But as we've done in the recent past Reds, let's not give them or the media the satisfaction by tainting the good reputation we've built up since the late '70s. We know we're no angels and we still have our fair share of snappers but if you care about the future of our game, don't you think it's about time we started building bridges instead or burning them?

Sing your hearts out for the lads in Europe and all over the UK, but let's try to get more converts in our ranks, eh lads, and that way we'll keep the red flag flying, forever.

... and the beat goes on. Glory, Glory Man United — with the FA Cup and Charity Shield, 1990

100% Reds: Andrei Kanchelskis and Brian McClair with even more silverware!
League Cup and European Super Cup, 1992

11

THE MOTHER OF ALL PARTIES

Have you ever prepared for a party for a special occasion? Well, you know the feeling of adrenalin pumping as the anticipation and excitement becomes too much the closer the big day gets. After the season of '92, we just knew our team couldn't blow it again, and this time we were ready. This party has been a long time coming, and boy oh boy were we ready for it.

A lot of fans took great pleasure and joy in seeing us miss out by chanting "Leeds" and "We've never seen United win the League" – not all clubs, just a few. Well they won't be chanting now, and we fans do have good memories and our day will come again. The players and management remember those games and really will show those two or three clubs how to play football the champion's way. The Red Army will overcome as we always do and keep the red flag flying high and give those envious fans a knowing smile of contentment.

Back in 1967, the club had a team of great individuals. They had their share of flair players, grafters, midfield generals, hard men and jokers and it's taken Fergie a few years to assemble this

Living legends: my boyhood heroes in 1967.

team. Though we were winning things in '90-'91 the fans felt there was just a little something missing – we were good, but not great. But after Rotterdam we know the team can function as a unit now, with the odd change here and there – as with Cantona and now Keane and in the future someone else, maybe from the youth "dream team" who knows.

But the nucleus of this team now are legends, and can be compared with the team of '67 right down to the final league table results.

The championship season is well documented and clear in most Reds' minds, but it was a nail biting time for all of us and we all have our different ideas of when we felt it was finally ours for the taking. Was it the signing of Eric Cantona, the Schmeichel saves against Villa and Liverpool, Lee Sharpe's return to the first team, Norwich away or Steve Bruce's headers against Sheffield Wednesday? Whichever was in your mind, you'll keep it as I will. Nobody can ever take that away and we can all smile like Cheshire cats every time we think of that moment.

I saw Villa and Norwich play some really good football over the season. They were worthy challengers and kept the race going all through the season, especially Norwich. We all feared Villa might steal it to a point, but the Canaries did a remarkable job. Nobody gave them a chance and I'm pleased they've got a European place after losing out back in '85.

Make or Break

For me *the feeling* hit me on the evening of April 5th away to Norwich. We could see for ourselves the make or break situation. The United battleship out-gunned the Norfolk cruiser in such a way their bows were under water before they knew what had hit them and there was no coming back. Like pirates they boarded, looted and left their Admiral of the fleet (Mike Walker) in total shock, from which they never really recovered. Fans all around were over the moon with that result but were still saying: "Now if they beat so and so and we get such a result etc.", but for me that was it, I had no doubts in my mind. Organise the party now.

Every member of the squad is a hero to the fans. But here again I have my own favourites. With the Frenchman Eric Cantona arriving, the media overkill was a bit OTT, when I and many others thought the return of Lee Sharpe was a

major factor to the form we were enjoying. *Ooh arrh* was exciting to watch as were Giggs and Hughes, and Ince and McClair, Bruce and Pally were at times marvellous.

Defenders and goalies too are often the unsung heroes as we all like to remember the goal scoring strikers, but Irwin, Parker and Big Peter all had games in which the fans in our vicinity thought each was Man of the Match. And that showed in the very last game of the season, where it meant every member of the squad scored a goal except Schmeichel. Older fans will remember Alex Stepney scoring two back in the '60s or '70s, so please take note Mr Ferguson. Seven straight wins in the run in, with goals from Kanchelskis, Dublin and Robson when it mattered completed the jigsaw to show some clubs that to be champions with style, the goals don't just come from one or two hit men.

Who will ever forget the Sheffield Wednesday game at OT? Roy of the Rovers had just retired but for all the world he was alive and kicking in spirit in the shape of Steve Bruce. Time was running out, United were behind 0-1. Would it be our day? It wasn't a make or break situation, but it was at a stage in the season where every point could have made the difference on May 9th.

When the referee Mr Peck pulled a muscle, the replacement linesman added on a full seven minutes. My mates and I were biting our nails, the team were still plugging away at the Owls' defences, then up popped Stevie Bruce to nod in Irwin's corner. As usual the OT crowd turned up the volume and those few final minutes everyone was looking at their watches wondering just when the ref would blow for the full time.

It was very very tense and then Pally knocked back another Giggsy corner and up popped the comic book hero – bang, a header I was right in line with. There was only one place that ball was going – in the back of the net. Steve Bruce aka Roy of the ...... was the hero of the day. Brian Kidd was on the field praying, Fergie was up off the bench, 40,000 plus Reds were exploding with delight and seconds later the final whistle blew. I crossed myself and said: "God bless Stevie Bruce". What a relief. My mates and I danced out of the Stretford End our hearts still pounding, adrenalin pumping and the talk on the way up Warwick Road was that Lady Luck was with us and this time our dreams have just got to come true.

In the car *Halfway to Paradise* by Billy Fury was playing on the radio, and we could see other Reds in the traffic jam had the same station on and were waving their arms around to the song. Very apt. Now every time I hear that song I will think to myself, God Bless Stevie Bruce and his two late goals.

Just for the record we know the battle for the championship was close right up into April and it was a good one, but in years to come the record books will show that in big Ron Atkinson's own words: "Villa's nerve went, and ours held and we won the league by 10 clear points and yet another first for Manchester United the 1st Premier League Champions" or MUFC Plc . . . get it?

Champions, Champions

By the time Villa were playing Oldham I had decided not to listen to it or watch it. That Sunday the family went to the park. Go round a car boot sale, a few beers in the local and watch a film after Sunday dinner and then 'er indoors decided to put the radio on in the kitchen and the last few minutes of Oldham's game was on.

I couldn't bring myself to listen to it, but the wife was relaying Tom Tyrell's words through the doorway. I'm shouting: "I don't wanna know, I don't wanna know, shut the door" and then with only 60 seconds left, I left the film and over the airwaves I could hear: "There's the whistle – Manchester United are the Premier League Champions". Yyyesss championés, championés are we, are we, are we.

The party was on, two games remained. Contingency plans had been made way back at the beginning of April for all the lads and our wives and kids to have a party when we had come back from Wimbledon, but all that changed. The party was still on but now we could celebrate at Old Trafford in style. But how the hell could one sleep that night having to wait 27 hours? There was only one thing for it, let's party now.

May 2nd, Sunday tea time, stories were coming through the grapevine, well BT actually. The pubs in town were going spare, United's Red Army was on the tiles, Piccadilly, Albert Square, Salford Precinct, cars were driving around horns blazing, fans and flags hanging out of the windows and everyone converging on OT. I was told when Tom Tyrell said those words on the radio in our kitchen over 100 cars were parked up on the double yellow lines outside the ground and they all simultaneously blew their horns and popped the champagne corks. Even Lee Sharpe

had gone down to the stadium to see the celebrations.

Manchester city centre became Manchester United Centre well into the night. 1.30 am and the Prince Albert memorial had a United ski hat on and rumour has it, his stone foot was tapping along with the ravers well into the early hours. An all nighter vigil was on down at the ground – when Mancunians party they really do it in style.

British summers can be unpredictable and Manchester's geographical position in the North West, where we are in a type of basin surrounded by hills on three sides, makes weather roll in and out from the Atlantic Ocean and Irish Sea like the tides at the seaside. But this morning of Monday the 3rd May was perfect – blue sky, the odd cloud, just a hint of warm breeze. Just as if someone up there knew that evening was going to be something special.

I was like a little boy waiting to get up Christmas morning to open his presents, and you can bet I wasn't the only one. While on the phone to one of my friend's wives she told me: "I haven't seen him like this since '68". It was for Manchester United fans a very special day – all over the world the Red Army was sending delegates from the crusades to the mecca of football – those lucky enough to have a ticket that is.

We could have filled the Maracana stadium itself no trouble, but the TV and satellite companies were beaming the game out to over 70 countries worldwide, so millions would be able to see the fantastic spectacle. Alex Ferguson refused all the fireworks and dancing girls on the pitch, usually connected with live satellite coverage. We didn't need it, we the fans could provide all the pre-match entertainment and we did.

I took the whole family and a neighbour down to the stadium, to take in some of the festivities. It was around 2pm and driving through Manchester it seemed that every other car had flags, scarfs and posters hanging from it. Taxi cabs had red and white streamers and even GM buses had red and white balloons and flags hanging from the windows and side mirrors. The Red Army was being drawn westward out of the city centre towards the "theatre of dreams".

I'm just glad all my family – mum, dad, sister, uncles, aunties, wife and daughter – were able to understand just what it was like to stand on that famous Stretford End before it was demolished. Because unless they've actually been down to the ground and felt the electricity created by players and supporters united in the common cause... to win, and win in style, they'll never understand.

My family do and though Old Trafford is now all-seater and the capacity is ridiculously low for a club with the support we have, the wife and daughter will just have to remember the Stretford End singing and swaying, the team winning and hope that a spare ticket becomes available in the future. Or the club does the decent thing and builds another tier on top of what we've already got.

Carnival

That afternoon we saw a carnival atmosphere never before seen down at that famous stadium. In 1967 and 1968 it was wonderful, but people were more reserved back then and more conservative in their dress. The crowds went mad singing and shouting with joy as they do today, and in the '70s Tommy Doc's tartan army was a sight to see. But the '90s have seen such things as face paints, outlandish designer clothes, colourful T shirts, replica kits and huge European style flags and banners. Put this lot together with the enthusiasm and ferver of the fans from the '60s and '70s and you'll get a picture of what it was like outside OT on that marvellous afternoon.

The players started to arrive around tea time as usual in their cars, only this time they needed a police escort to get through the delighted partying fans tapping on the windows and roofs trying to get a glimpse, or photo of their heroes. One by one they were cheered into the forecourt, every inch of the way being mobbed. When Fergie and Kiddo arrived it was like two world champion prize fighters entering the arena with body guards and security all around them. The fans' arms were outstretched in a frenzied mass all trying to congratulate the manager and his assistant, just as I had done as a lad to the great man back in the '60s. It was a marvellous sight.

The off licences on Chester Road were unloading the beer at the back door and it was being passed directly to the fans queuing at the counters at the front of the shops without even a sniff of being stacked on the shelves. All the pubs for miles around the stadium were packed to the doors and then some. The coaches were pouring into Trafford Park from all routes North and South. I would have loved to have had some aerial shots with my camera from the police helicopter circling above. It was some 25 hours

after Oldham's victory over Villa and the party was still in full swing.

Everybody was well oiled as they say but I noticed not many were going OTT because nobody wanted to miss the evening's festivities inside the stadium later on. And besides, with the sun beating down the beer was just evaporating as it went down – we just kept on going. My mates and I had downed a few bottles of Lanson Black Label and Moet Chandon champagne and the Boddingtons was virtually on tap.

The masses had gathered and it was time to go into the ground and revel with the rest of the Red Army assembled under the blue and pink dusky skies above the "theatre of dreams". This was the moment we had waited 26 long years for. Although the Stretford End wasn't fully redeveloped my mates and I were overjoyed – we had been able to get our seats as soon as it had reopened. Old Trafford was like one massive karaoke club – the whole stadium was rockin'.

Down to business. As the gladiators entered the arena the volume of noise was deafening as "Champions, Champions" rang around the stadium. It seemed everyone was just settling in when Kevin Gallacher scored – a neat, near ball cross in the ninth minute. For a few seconds we could hear ourselves think, but, what the hell, we were champions and the party resumed – we were sure our team wouldn't let this one slip. It was carnival time and if this atmosphere couldn't lift them, nothing would. It was as if they needed this reminder to get themselves going.

It didn't take long for the lads to get into the swing of things – just 13 minutes to be exact. A free kick at the Scoreboard End and a chance for Georgie, er, I mean Ryan to show off his skills. A swerving shot, that the keeper and the rest of us thought the defensive wall had covered, flew into the net and the young silent assassin's face was agog as he flew like an eagle, arms outstretched towards the fans behind the goal who at this point were going crazy with delight.

Incy later put United in front latching on to a through ball that the Frenchman Cantona had measured perfectly – 2-1 to us. And as had happened a few times in the season, Incy and Giggs had a little celebratory jig of their own to delight any dance floor Manchester has to offer. We've all read comparisons with Best and Giggs, but to see the young Welsh International flying down the wing juggling the ball along, without it touching the floor doesn't half take you back a bit.

The game passed so quickly – none of us

May 3rd 1993 at O.T. turned out to be May Day for Blackburn and flag day for the Reds.

Ooh la, la . . . Stretford Enders go 'Allo, Allo'

wanted it to end – and when in the very last minute United got a free kick at the Stretford End on the edge of the box we all held our breath. Cameras were at the ready – who would take it? Robbo, Irwin? No the big man just stepped up and smacked it right into the corner, bloody hell, it was Pally, Gary Pallister had scored!

What a fitting end to a game – the 89th minute goal brought the broadest smile I had ever seen on the big yin's face. No disrespect intended Pally, but he doesn't always look the most comfortable and relaxed player on the field. I don't mean in his skill, I mean his facial expressions sometimes look like the lad's in pain – but not that night.

After the match, celebrations began with Bryan Robson and Steve Bruce as club and team captains going up to collect the brand new Premier League trophy together. On the team's lap of honour it seemed like a million flash bulbs were popping all over the night sky and for once it was nice to see the media were kept from swarming on to the field as they do so often spoiling the fan's enjoyment. A lap of honour should be just that: a special moment for the players and fans.

It was also nice to see the lads' faces all joyful

and the gleaming new trophy without 101 photographers swarming all over the team fighting to get the Pulitzer Prize or whatever for the most intrusive photo. These guys have got lenses that could pick out a needle in a haystack at 40,000 feet, so why do they spoil the occasion and the chance for a few fans to get their own personal snap they will cherish forever?

"We are the champions" rang out as we left the stadium into the darkness – a mass of red and white and green and gold flags. Someone suggested our old Newton Heath colours may have been a bit of a hoodoo because they didn't bring the boys of 1878 much luck. But all that fell through at the Crystal Palace away game and everyone was sporting the new look.

It did seem a bit unusual at first but anything is better than the horrible sky blue banners and scarfs they were trying to sell us at Wembley in the Forest League Cup Final. I just refuse to acknowledge anything sky blue some sponsors have come up with, even though it was a very popular fashion accessory. It's the best selling football shirt Adidas have ever sold I believe – but it's not for me, red is my colour.

Back at the celebrations, Piccadilly Gardens in Manchester was full of singing, dancing supporters. All those off licences that had earlier made a killing were totally sold out, the pubs were changing kegs like nobody's business and the mother of all parties was still going strong and went on well into the night. I bid my friends a fond farewell and got on to the Metro tram with loads of other smiling Reds' faces, some still not believing what was truly, finally ours. It was the crown that was put on Robbo's head for all the world to see.

When I got home, the wife and a few neighbours and friends who had come round, had organised a little extra celebration. She'd made a championship cake and yet a few more bottles of bubbly and beer were opened. Though we all had work to go to the next morning, the party was now well into its 31st hour and still rockin. Needless to say I had a bad bead in the morning, but nothing was going to stop me from going into work to see the old Blue nose (city fan) eat humble pie.

It's terrible what envy can make some people say and I had to take a lot of stick over last season's disappointment. So I went in head held high sporting my new Fergies Red and White Trophies T-shirt with pride and surprisingly enough the Blues at work sportingly congratulated me and my team for winning in style. To say the least, I was taken aback and though now we are back to our usual mickey-taking rivalry, at the time it was appreciated. You see we're not all bad. Well done you true Blues – if only the others could follow suit we would all get along a lot better.

The last game of the season was at Wimbledon. The thing was, Villa were away to QPR and we were sharing the same stretch of motorway. Well, what a contrast in passengers – inevitable really but all credit to those Midlanders who were brave enough to travel down and follow their team knowing our paths were bound to cross at some stage on the journey south.

As we were celebrating, all the old fancy dress outfits were out – Fred Flintstone, Mr Blobby, Quasi etc. As usual the Met couldn't organise themselves to find a can of Boddies in the Boddingtons factory. It was utter chaos outside. There were either a lot of forged tickets about or the men on the turnstiles were coining it in. Either way there were far too many fans in that ground and a lot more than the official gate of 30,115.

The team signed off with a 2-1 win with goals from Ince and Robbo, Captain Marvell himself, back with the captain's arm band on. The ball had been put through by Stevie Bruce who had been a magnificent team captain himself. It was all topped off with a streaker and a meaningless pitch invasion – more in the way of a celebration than any other reason and it was after the final whistle.

We left for the off licence and didn't hang around – it was party time, remember. But we did see a Wombles fan there honest – they are not a myth I promise you. On the journey home we did see some smiling faces heading North, the odd mini bus and car load of Wycombe Wanderers supporters who had won at Wembley against Runcorn and at the services some lads swapped scarves and hats and the day's stories.

The party was now seven days and six hours old. All our wives and children and a few friends had kept the date of our originally planned celebration and with a United music tape on the go, even after a long day in the smoke (London) we were finishing off the final bottle of Bells, the cake, quiche, rolls and chicken, and the remnants of the beer was hitting the kitchen bin like slam dunking a basketball. And as they say, that was it, the party was over – 176 hours in all. Some party eh?...till the next time.

Ain't no stopping it now . . . as Ince's shot heads for goal.

Seconds later, Ince and Giggs . . . let's boogie!

12

LONG LIVE THE LEGEND

Since the days of old, back in '67 we've been this close on many occasions to the Holy Grail, the championship. We've seen marvellous and momentous occasions pass through time, such things that we'll never forget but which to some are a distant memory. We've seen the QE2's maiden voyage, the first flight Concorde, the Berlin wall come and go, two wars – in the Falklands and the Gulf. Least of all, the end of the Cold War and demise of communism

We wouldn't have had thousands of United fans visiting Moscow back in '67. Man landed on the moon and now has shuttle trips into space. We've found out one of the great train robbers is a Red. Pop groups come and go – the Beatles, Slade, Queen. Fashions have spun around at least twice. The mods in the '60s had a revival in the late '70s. We've had two waves of skinheads '69 and '77 and the '70s themselves are back in vogue with Abba and platform shoes. The Queen's Jubilee, Prince Charles' fairy tale wedding that has long since turned into a nightmare – so many things have changed, political, manmade and natural disasters.

The world doesn't stop for football, but it often seemed that time had stood still for many of Manchester United's footballers. The champions of 1967 became legends in their own right, but the longer we went without emulating their famous victory the heavier the burden became for every single player who arrived through the main entrance of Old Trafford.

The banner says it all: Wembley '83

Oh yes, we've had some marvellous and wonderful victories in Cup and European competitions but the Holy Grail is the one these crusades have been all about. At last, every single one of us can relax – the players, the management team and, of course, we the fans can proudly sprout two massive fingers up to those envious and spiteful clubs who took great pleasure in seeing us miss out in '92.

Throughout this book we've tried to put across a positive image and tried not to incite any ill feeling among all supporters, but we just can't understand the intensity by what was only two or three sets of supporters, behaving unsportingly in that way. It can only be put down to envy and jealousy because Manchester United are and always will be the biggest and best club in this country, regardless of whether we win something every season or we have to wait another decade.

All the aggro in the world won't change that, so wouldn't it be better if we all appreciated one another's teams in the traditional way? There's nothing wrong with healthy rivalry and taking the mickey out of each other at work or down the pub. But we must try and learn to get on together before another shameful disaster occurs in the name of sport.

The crusades have taken over two and a half decades to recapture the coveted Holy Grail. At times it was too much to bear for some players and managers. They've all come and gone, broken down and cried, got injured, sacked or retired, grown old trying to succeed. But we the fans have stood by our team helping them in their quest –

something the board and chairman should seriously take into consideration.

They must show us, the fans, they don't take us for granted by keeping entrance fees within the working class man's pocket and campaign to reduce transfer fees for players. Only then will those who profess to run this game command respect from the general public. Until the greed stops they haven't got a cat in hell's chance. But will they ever listen? I doubt it.

Like knights of old, we the fans have at times been chivalrous, loyal and courageous, sometimes ruthless in the common cause as foot soldiers joining the crusades over these long, long years. And in those years we've come up against some mighty foes, fought with and slayed some sworn enemies and fearsome monsters, travelled the world over seeking the right calibre of player to help us find the Grail.

The crusades began in '67 with the legendary great man (Sir Matt), his king (Law), his general (Charlton) and the mystical genius (Best), guards (Foulkes, Stiles, Crerand). They all went to the south lands and did combat with the claret and blue knight with the crossed hammers – he got ironed out 6 bouts to 1. More great victories were won throughout Europe in '68. First Malta fell – staunch allies ever since – followed by the Slavs, Poles and the Spanish who we have conquered on many auspicious occasions.

Then one knight appeared who we all feared and respected . . . the "black pearl" (Eusabio). The bouts were fierce and at one point the great man walked among his tired and weary troops (extra

Left: 1967. Right: 1993. Note the amazing similarity in the tables. Won 24, drawn 12, lost 6.

DIVISION 1 1966-1967	P	W	D	L	F	A	W	D	L	F	A	Pts
MANCHESTER U	42	17	4	0	51	13	7	8	6	33	32	60
Nottingham F	42	16	4	1	41	13	7	6	8	23	28	56
Tottenham H	42	15	3	3	44	21	9	5	7	27	27	56
Leeds U	42	15	4	2	41	17	7	7	7	21	25	55
Liverpool	42	12	7	2	36	17	7	6	8	28	30	51
Everton	42	11	4	6	39	22	8	6	7	26	24	48
Arsenal	42	11	6	4	32	20	5	8	8	26	27	46
Leicester C	42	12	4	5	47	28	6	4	11	31	43	44
Chelsea	42	7	9	5	33	29	8	5	8	34	33	44
Sheffield U	42	11	5	5	34	22	5	5	11	18	37	42
Sheffield W	42	9	7	5	39	19	5	6	10	17	28	41
Stoke C	42	11	5	5	40	21	6	2	13	23	37	41
WBA	42	11	1	9	40	28	5	6	10	37	45	39
Burnley	42	11	4	6	43	28	4	5	12	23	48	39
Manchester C	42	8	9	4	27	25	4	6	11	16	27	39
West Ham U	42	8	6	7	40	31	6	2	13	40	53	36
Sunderland	42	12	3	6	39	26	2	5	14	19	46	36
Fulham	42	8	7	6	49	34	3	5	13	22	49	34
Southampton	42	10	3	8	49	41	4	3	14	25	51	34
Newcastle U	42	9	5	7	24	27	3	4	14	15	54	33
Aston Villa	42	7	5	9	30	33	4	2	15	24	52	29
Blackpool	42	1	5	15	18	36	5	4	12	23	40	21

United's leading League goalscorer: Law 23

FA PREMIER LEAGUE 1992-93		P	W	D	L	F	A	Pts
1	Manchester United	42	24	12	6	67	31	84
2	Aston Villa	42	21	11	10	57	40	74
3	Norwich City	42	21	9	12	61	65	72
4	Blackburn Rovers	42	20	11	11	68	46	71
5	Queens Park Rangers	42	17	12	13	63	55	63
6	Liverpool	42	16	11	15	62	55	59
7	Sheffield Wednesday	42	15	14	13	55	51	59
8	Tottenham Hotspur	42	16	11	15	60	66	59
9	Manchester City	42	15	12	15	56	51	57
10	Arsenal	42	15	11	16	40	38	56
11	Chelsea	42	14	14	14	51	54	56
12	Wimbledon	42	14	12	16	56	55	54
13	Everton	42	15	8	19	53	55	53
14	Sheffield United	42	14	10	18	54	53	52
15	Coventry City	42	13	13	16	52	57	52
16	Ipswich Town	42	12	16	14	50	55	52
17	Leeds United	42	12	15	15	57	62	51
18	Southampton	42	13	11	18	54	61	50
19	Oldham	42	13	10	19	63	74	49
20	Crystal Palace	42	11	16	15	48	61	49
21	Middlesbrough	42	11	11	20	54	75	44
22	Nottingham Forest	42	10	10	22	41	62	40

time team talk) and gave them words of encouragement that inspired them to find inner strength and defeat the Eagles from Portugal. That night another young man, gallant and fearless, came into his own on his 19th birthday, taking two stabs at the Portuguese knights' defence. Oh, how we all danced and sang his praises (Kiddo) and bravery.

The elders of the Kingdom (directors of Manchester United) called in the Doc (Tommy) to patch up the wounds dealt by our old enemy and foes (City) and he in turn enlisted other brave chivalrous knights to carry on the crusades and the search for that elusive Holy Grail. Merlin himself (Hill) enlisted as did another wing wizard (Coppell) and a giant of a warrior standing six foot two with eyes of blue (Holton). The knights of old (Trafford) never seemed to lose a battle while he was by our side, but injury – cursed upon him by evil doers – meant he was sent to Coventry.

We rampaged through the 2nd division. The Mexican (Pancho) Pearson had a salute of his own, like the king of '67 (Law) which he gave many times, sending the foot soldiers into raptures and emulating his mannerisms among ourselves on the playing fields and beaches all over Europe. Like King Richard the Lionheart's crusade, none of us knew just how long they would last. We had sightings of the Grail many times. The brothers (Greenhoff) and the new general – the iceman (Buchan) had arrived. More Celtic warriors fearsome by nature joined our ranks: Macari – nippy and elegant, McQueen – noble, and a dangerous dark knight – Joe Jordan. He made Vlad the Impailer look like Andy Pandy – with a killer instinct so strong he scared the crap out of his own kind at the training camp.

It seems we have a history of conquering foes that have a bird emblem on their shields: Golden Eagle (Benfica) '68, Liver Bird (Liverpool) '77, '79, '85 etc., Seagulls (Brighton) '83 and Bald Eagle (C. Palace) '90.

Among some of the most famous knights who have attended the court of the round table (manager's office), we've had our share of court jesters (Roache, Anderson, Milne) to entertain the troops. But there is not one foot soldier among us who, just for one day, would not swap our lowly surf's position to try on that suit of armour (Utd shirt) and be a gallant knight with golden haired damsels falling at our feet with love and praise in their bosom.

The man from the far north (Fergie) with glare of steel and, we are lead to believe, temper of the Viking god Thor, has in the '90s assembled a fighting force the likes of which we haven't seen in our Kingdom (Manchester United) since the knights of old (Trafford) paraded the mythical "grail" here back in '67. We know it exists, but it's been that long since we saw it, rumour was, some fire breathing lamb eating dragon had buried it so deep upon the moors it would never be found. As with most myths, this was not true.

With a string of great victories behind him, our leader (Fergie) was trusted and admired. After a shaky start to the present campaign, the foot soldiers of Ferguson's red and white army were asked to once again look for the Grail overseas, and with his general (Robson), a flyer (Sharpe), a priceless fighter with the name the guvnor (Ince), a menacing stopper (Sealey), our own fire breathing dragon (Hughesie) and 30,000 crusaders, we took on the might of one of Europe's most feared fighting machines (Barcelona). Our leader not only tactically out fought the Dutchmen (Cruyf) and co but another hero of the hour, he of the suntanned legs (Blackmore), saved our rear guard and two unstoppable thrusts, with sparks flying (Hughesie), put the bout beyond the Spaniard's reach.

After 25 years we had battled our way across continents in search of this most coveted trophy and won everything in our land that was possible to win: European Cup '68, the FA Cup '90, the Charity Shield 90/93, E.C.W. Cup '91, European Super Cup '91, League Cup '92 and the FA Youth Cup '92, yet the one trophy we had all been searching for all these years seemed to be lost.

But just then in a flash of blinding light (a BT phone call actually) a message came through to our leader that a Frenchman had not only seen the Grail, but had actually had his hands on it. How could anybody who had been so close to it not join our quest? And having seen it once, the French Lieutenant could not resist the chance to behold its glorious sight once more and along he came. "Ooh arh!" we cried, "Ooh arh, Cantona".

The Viking (Schmeichel) a giant of a man was voted best of his kind (goalie) in the world. We had a brave and fearless new team captain (Bruce) alongside club captain and general (Robson). A red knight (Kanchelskis) had also arrived to join the crusades and last but not least a young man we foot soldiers had seen rise from surf (youth team) to knight in shining armour (first team) – none other than the silent assassin himself (Ryan Giggs), the fastest most skilfully talented knight we have seen in our kingdom since the mystical genius (Best) over 20 years ago.

There were great conquests throughout the '93 campaign especially the ones against Leeds Sept 6th, Oldham Nov 21st, City Dec 6th, Sheffield Wednesday Dec 26th, Spurs Jan 9th, Liverpool March 5th, Norwich April 5th, Coventry April 12th and the unforgettable Crystal Palace game April 21st. But the day that will go down in history for every single member of the all conquering Red Army is Monday May 3rd 1993, the 3-1 victory over Blackburn Rovers. This was the day the coveted Holy Grail finally came back home and we unashamedly wept with joy as it was paraded around the "theatre of dreams". It is one that will never be forgotten.

I just hope my children and grand children don't have to wait another 26 years. I'd hate to go through all that again, but I'm sure there will be no shortage of loyal volunteers to do so if we were ever in a similar situation. If the cause is a worthy one, we the people won't ever be found wanting in the common cause to bring the biggest and best trophies to the theatre of dreams and would give our full support to the future knights (players) of Manchester United.

LONG LIVE THE LEGEND – LONG LIVE MUFC.

Previous Premiership Meetings

Team	Won	Drawn	Lost
Arsenal	61	33	56
Aston Villa	53	28	41
Blackburn Rovers	26	17	23
Chelsea	46	27	29
Coventry City	26	15	18
Everton	47	33	50
Ipswich Town	19	8	16
Leeds United	26	27	19
Liverpool	42	38	42
Manchester City	44	44	32
Newcastle United	50	27	35
Norwich City	25	12	9
Oldham Athletic	17	9	10
Queens Park Rangers	19	9	6
Sheffield United	39	15	33
Sheffield Wed.	44	22	34
Southampton	30	19	18
Swindon Town	1	1	0
Tottenham H'spur	50	32	32
West Ham United	32	17	33
Wimbledon	8	4	5

(as at 30.3.94)

Table above: the total previous meetings against Manchester United since 1878. By the end of the 93/94 season, let's hope at least three of them change in our favour – read 'em and weep boys.

Simply the best – legends of 1993

13

THE REDS GO MARCHING ON! ON! ON!

Well – it wasn't 26 years, not even 26 months – in fact, it doesn't seem like 26 hours since we were all dancing in the street and reds were rocking all over the world.

Will Fergie's team stay together? Bringing in more English players for European ties will mean someone's for the chop, but who? Why break up a winning formula? I'll bet many of you out there would love to see the championship winning team play in Europe – the ones who have grafted hard and consistently produced memorable football. This is what the public want to see. I don't care whether A.C. Milan have Dutch, German or Spanish players by the score, I'd put United's full squad up against anybody because when they play at their best, they are capable of beating anyone.

What we don't want, but have been lumbered with, is having to see our club put out half a team with players playing out of position and inexperienced reserves doing their best for one or two games. To win the best trophies you've got to play your best team – here endeth the lesson.

So many things have happened in this 93/94 season and, as with all the other stories in the book, I can only give you a glimpse of our most memorable matches and how we followed Manchester United and the red army on tour.

Play Your Best Team

The F.A. Charity Shield versus Arsenal on August 7th was revenge for the South African tour defeat when we lost on two penalties. It was a lovely sunny August afternoon, and the game itself was nothing much to shout about apart from two very good strikes from Ian Wright of Arsenal and Mark

Hughes of United. But the penalty shoot-out was nail-biting stuff and had a peculiar twist to the end. The players take five penalties each and, if it's still a draw after that, it's sudden death to the first team to miss.

Now this is where it gets a bit complicated. First up to the spot was Paul Ince, no problem – bang, 1-0; Winterburn, accompanied by deafening whistling around the stadium scored to silence the crowd, 1-1; Steve Bruce, who used to be our penalty taker before Eric, made it 2-1 to United. Jenson made it 2-2, but then Denis Irwin missed. Campbell made it 2-3 to Arsenal, then the new boy from Nottingham Forest, Roy "Keano" Kean, rammed one in to make it 3-3, followed by Merson for 3-4 to the Gunners. But Ooh! Aah! Cantona! cheekily side-footed one into the bottom right-hand corner, Seaman didn't even move from his standing position, it flew in to make it 4-4. Arsenal hero Ian Wright, strode up to the spot but he shot wide. It was still 4-4 and sudden death, and if there was anybody we could depend on it was Captain Marvel. Robbo obliged by making it 5-4 to United and we were surprised when Seaman volunteered. It was goalie versus goalie, but Peter Schmeichel saved it and it was all over. The team celebrated with the first piece of silverware of the four they would eventually contend

The Sunset Sharpy Shuffle

Villa away was, this season, a bit further away for me than the 80 miles or so from Manchester to Birmingham. We were in Spain on a family vacation but managed to see the boys live on Spanish satellite TV in the evening sunset. Half the British ex-patriots in the area set up the chairs cinema fashion outside the bar we had chosen. A great time was had by all and when Lee Sharpe scored his goals against the Villa on a huge video screen up on the wall it was to a backdrop of a pink, amber and purple sky and the sound of the waves breaking upon the shore. I still remember the sight of the lads imitating the Sharpy Shuffle, then leaping into the open air swimming pool alongside the bar where Lee's goals were being re-played in glorious Technicolor.

September saw us back on the European trail and our club has a proud record in the champions competition. We've never lost a home tie at OT and have always reached the semi-final since 1957. Sir Matt took the boys to four semi-finals and a final in '57, '58, '66, '68 and '69. This time, the reds were 3-2 winners with goals from Keane and Cantona.

In October, we had the League Cup second round against Stoke City. Lou Macari still has a chippy on Chester Road and said that if Stoke won that evening, every customer would get free fish and chips. Lee Sharpe must have fancied raw steak that night, because he was like a lion pouncing on the Christians. They didn't stand a chance and, just at the start of the second half, he scored a brilliant scissor-kick volley. When Hughes put Chocky through and he smashed it into the net to make it 2-0 (3-2 on agg) we knew we'd go without any supper that evening.

QPR were the next team to be steam-rollered into submission. Here, we were thirteen games into the season and still top of the league. Winning 2-1 just three days after despatching Leicester City 5-1 seemed miraculous, but Eric Cantona's solo goal against the blue and white hoops was even better then the free kick goal he scored against Arsenal.

Welcome To Hell

November: many reds feel we only have ourselves to blame for our exit from the European Cup after being 2-0 up against the Turkish side Galatasaray. Somehow, we let it slip having to rely on Cantona to come up trumps to keep our unbeaten record at OT with a 3-3 draw. The fences at OT were lowered due to our recent record of good crowd behaviour but an invasion of the pitch by two Kurdish refugees burning a Turkish flag infuriated big Peter Schmeichel and he unceremoniously ejected one of them from the pitch by the scruff of his neck.

Some of my pals went to the away leg and I was offered a last minute flight ticket. Luckily for me, I couldn't join them. I heard later about the horrific scenes right from the word go: at the airport, the team and the fans were subjected to provocation; cars and vans cut up the traffic taking the fans to their hotel; and we all remember reading of the fans who were deported without even seeing the match and those with legitimate tickets getting to their seats only to find them taken up by Turkish security and their fellow supporters. As for the game, I can't ever remember my team not having a single attempt on goal in such an important game. Many say Mark Hughes should have played or we blew it after being 2-0 up at Old Trafford in the first leg or the foreign player rule worked against us. Who knows.

Derby Day at Maine Road was just days after the Galatasaray game. City were 2-0 up at half time and the blue noses were very generous in offering us Turkish Delights – nice one – but Eric the red and Keano had other ideas. When the score-line read 3-2 to United we ate our chocolate bars with relish. Yet again we danced down Wilmslow Road towards the city centre singing the praises of Ooh! Aah! Cantona!

December saw a 1-1 away draw with Newcastle. Paul Ince put us into the lead, but Andy Cole got the Magpies equaliser fair enough.

Heaven 1, Man United 0

January 20th 1994 – The man we thought was indestructible, Sir Matt Busby, passed away. The great man who had had the last rites said over him on no less than three occasions finally left us aged 84 and went to join his babes. We all have our own personal memories of Sir Matt and we will never forget what he did for this club. He was respected by all in football, and the club received messages of condolences from all over the world. By the time of the Saturday game versus Everton, they had grown into a sea of red and white wreaths and football memorabilia. There were tributes laid from Red Star Belgrade, Moscow, A C Milan, Real Madrid and many others.

On the day of the game against Everton, the president of UEFA, Lennart Johansson, and delegates from the Football League and the F.A. were at Old Trafford. Inside the stadium there was total silence – you could have heard a pin drop as a lone piper led out the two teams playing the Scottish lament "The Green Hills of Tyrol".

The Everton fans acted impeccably. The teams brushed their tears aside, and pride filled out hearts as we roared on the team. Ryan Giggs swept around defenders, which would have made the old boss happy. Ince, Cantona and the rest of the squad did it the Busby way with passion, flair and entertaining football.

On the day of the funeral it poured down as if the angels couldn't contain their tears, yet tens of thousands turned out and stood patiently in the torrential rain for hours. The cortege of limousines wound its way through the streets of Old Trafford, where it stopped for two minutes on Sir Matt Busby Way before resuming its journey to the cemetery for the Busby family to lay the great man finally to rest.

Trio Of Treats

The goals scored in the QPR and Wimbledon away matches on February 5th and 20th were some of the best seen on *Match of the Day*. The first was by Ryan Giggs: from the half-way line he just glided past one late tackle after another. Another in the same game was a 16-pass move culminating in Denis Irwin saying "anything you can do I can do better". The last of the trio came from Cantona in the away tie of the F.A. cup v Wimbledon. His volley in this game was another one for the video collection of goals of the season.

We Only Need Ten Men

Beware the ides of March. How true. This was the worst part of the whole season, with Peter Schmeichel being sent off in the game against Charlton Athletic in the F.A. Cup 6th round just before half time. We eventually won 3-1 singing "ten men, we only need ten men". We didn't think referees around the country would take that literally and, in following games, Cantona and Kanchelskis would take an early bath and Ince, Hughes and Keane were only a cat's whisker away from enforced match bans. Fergie had to mix 'n' match players for the next few games but still nobody could budge us from the top spot.

April: After two visits to Wembley already this season United fans were unhappy to hear that the F.A. had decided that two teams in the North of England less than 20 miles apart should play their semi-final tie at Wembley.

You Have to Earn It

Watching Mark Hughes get the equaliser, with 40 seconds to go against Oldham on T.V. wasn't ideal. The replay at Maine Road was, as they say a formality, a clear 4-1 win and the chant went up "one chance, you only get one chance", with goals from Irwin, Kanchelskis, Robson and Giggs.

Don't Worry, Be Happy!

The run-in to the end of the season was only five games away from a back-to-back premiership title, but first we had some nail-biting fixtures to face. There was the Derby against Manchester City, who had been fighting to stay out of the relegation area (what's new?) plus away games against Leeds and Ipswich who were just under City in the table and needed all the points they could get. So three very difficult games ahead in just over a week.

Enter, Monsieur Eric Cantona, returning after his five match ban. It was Derby Day at OT and he scored two easy-peasy goals my grandma could have side-footed in. We went home that day 2-0 winners. With Leeds we needn't have worried with two brilliant one-two passes which both included Hughsie, Kanchelskis and Giggs.

May 1st. Ipswich Town is a mighty long journey from OT but wherever the red devils play, along goes the mighty red army (when we can get a decent ticket allocation). Cantona was on form this day, covering every blade of grass and dragging defenders out of position left, right and centre then heading down a cross from Kanchelskis into the bottom corner of the net. The young lads on the terraces have adopted him as their new King of the Stretford End.

As for the *L'Enfant Terrible* tag, Eric has proved his critics wrong. Forget Vinny Jones' video nasty, dig out of your library the 1968 tie in the World Club Championships v Estudiantes. It was a miracle George Best survived. Nobby Stiles had a tooth knocked out and Denis Law had to have stitches in his knee. So next time Eric gets some stick, drown them out by cheering him on.

The other goal that afternoon was slid in by a flying Ryan Giggs; if our Lancashire neighbours slipped up this was the result that did it. We won the championship without having to kick another ball and with games to spare. The Ipswich fans invaded their pitch, calling for the head of their manager but then they came down to our corner and applauded our fans and our club. Any fans willing to build bridges with warm handshakes and wanting to swap scarves are okay by me.

The last two games at OT, against Southampton and Coventry were won in a carnival atmosphere. It was Bryan Robson's final curtain-call after 13 years. He has helped Manchester United become the standard bearers of what all the rest of the premiership clubs should set their sights on. Our Merseyside neighbours used to hold that honour but we are the current kings of the castle.

Things Can Only Get Better

MAY 14th – F.A. CUP FINAL DAY. There are few things finer than a North v South cup final and, as Chelsea were the only team to do the double over us in the league this season, we were looking forward to the game with the Prime Minister's team.

Some of the lads went to the final by coach, some by train and we would meet up the next day to tell our tales of the day's events. Some had

difficulty finding a boozer to get into without bouncers on the door and some unknowingly stumbled into a gay bar before ending up at the usual Wembley haunts – *The Torch* and *The Greyhound*.

It really was a game of two halves. Chelsea's player-manager Glenn Hoddle, no stranger to the big occasion, may have thought that his team with Gavin Peacock was due some divine intervention when the blue blade beat Schmeichel with a superb volley which struck the crossbar. But in the second half Eric – who else – slotted two divine rights into the net thanks to two penalty decisions given by referee David Elleray. Sparky Hughes mopped up an error by the Chelsea defence. The rain showered off the nets as the ball spun round in the back of the corner before it came to a halt – 3-0 up in nine minutes and we were singing "we've done the double". Chocky came on and was gifted a ball from Paul Ince and all Brian McClair had to do was side foot it in to make it 4-0.

Steve Bruce went up the steps to collect the cup on the team's behalf and I'm sure Bryan Robson wouldn't begrudge him that honour. As the team did their lap of honour, how fitting, an ear-piercing roar rang around the rafters BUSBY, BUSBY, BUSBY, to the great man's memory. I'm sure Alex Ferguson, Brian Kidd and both players and fans alike will keep the red flag flying high for many years to come.